# Noisy Contemplation

*Deep Prayer for Busy People*

OTHER PUBLICATIONS FROM QUIXOTE CENTER

The Inclusive Bible – The First Egalitarian Translation · 2007

Inclusive Language Lectionaries · 2008

Rivers of Hope · 2007

Let Haiti Live · 2004

Rome Has Spoken · 1998

Honduras: A Look at the Reality · 1985

El Salvador: A Look at the Reality · 1984

Nicaragua: A Look at the Reality · 1983

Karen Silkwood: Union Sister · 1978

OTHER PUBLICATIONS BY WILLIAM R. CALLAHAN

Agenda for Justice (w. Henriot & Ryan), Center of Concern · 1972

Soundings (ed.), Center of Concern · 1974

The Wind Is Rising, Quixote Center · 1978

Jason and Clytemnestra, Quixote Center · 1983

# Noisy Contemplation

*Deep Prayer for Busy People*

WILLIAM R. CALLAHAN

Quixote Center
Brentwood, Maryland
2008

Revised edition
ISBN 978-0-9795169-0-0

115,000 copies in eight printings

To encourage use of this book in workshops and study
groups, generous bulk quantity discounts are available from
Quixote Center. To order additional copies of this book,
you can:

- call toll-free:  800 746 1160
- use the order form at the back of this book
- visit quixote.org on the Web

Book and cover design by Andy Laken
Cover illustration by Vickie Reeves

Typeset, printed and bound in the USA.

To Susan,

May you see the Southwest with contemplative eyes.

Bill

# Dedication

To the people of the church, the Good News of Jesus, whose love for God and for each other witnesses our faith and brings hope for justice and peace upon our earth.

To the families of my growing, the Murphys and the Callahans. Thank you for your care and support.

To my Jesuit brothers of many years sharing, especially John Post, Bill Guindon and Paul Lucey, whose trust and friendship have been a blessing.

To two friends from heaven, Julia Immaculata, SND and Ellen Patricia, SND, for showing me what "merry" means.

To the people of Nicaragua who, since the first edition was published, taught me to dream in the midst of poverty and to forgive in the midst of pain.

To the present and past staff of the Quixote Center, in whose soil these dreams of justice and deep prayer have flourished. My special thanks to Maureen Fiedler, SL, for long friendship and collaboration, and to Dolly Pomerleau, who co-initiated the Center with me and whose spirit and friendship continue to touch my life.

# Acknowledgments

This work is the creation of many people, evolved over years of reflection. Many people, especially those who have shared workshops, have stimulated these ideas. But special thanks should go to those who helped draw the work together. More than twenty friends waded through the manuscript when it was "less than polished." What life it now possesses is a tribute to their creative critiques.

Special thanks to St. Ignatius Loyola, who dreamed that Jesuits could be "contemplatives in action." This volume dreams that noisy contemplation is possible for every follower of Jesus. A blessing to all who helped the dream find words and who make such prayer a lived reality.

This paperback edition exists because Dolly Pomerleau took time from a crowded schedule to supervise and shepherd the entire process of revision and publication. My thanks to Ellen Lynch, csc, Rose Marie Canty, csc and Jerry Pederson for assisting in proofing and planning the publication. Thanks to Andy Laken of the Quixote Center who designed and typeset this revised edition.

Special thanks to Jack Engel whose encouragement and critical reading of the original text moved this project from a wish to a reality.

# Contents

Foreword · 1

Introduction · 3

1 Stories of Pray-ers · 7

2 Jesus: His Life, Ministry and Prayer · 15

3 How Are We Called to Live? · 33

4 Marks of Healthy Prayer · 39

5 Prayer and Contemplation · 51

6 Redescribing Prayer and Pray-ers · 59

7 Noisy Contemplation: The Tools We Use · 65

8 Building Habits of Noisy Contemplation · 73

9 Prayer Apart: The Prayer of Perspective · 81

10 Contemplating the Earth and Civilization · 89

11 Contemplating People · 95

12 Contemplating Ourselves · 111

13 Contemplating God · 117

14 Contemplating Society: Loving Distant Neighbors · 129

15 Contemplation and Conflict · 147

16 Spiritual Direction for People of Few Resources · 157

17 Merry Prayer · 163

Conclusion · 169

# Foreword

"THIS APPROACH TO prayer is like the process of adapting plants to a broader range of growing conditions…What we now seek are new, vigorous varieties of prayer which can yield a fruitful harvest of deep contemplation for the home gardeners of our community." Thus concluded my 1978 article on "Noisy Contemplation" in *The Wind Is Rising*.

Like a gardener who plants the same varieties, but experiments with a few new seeds each year, this book enlarges and pushes beyond the insights of that article.

Since noisy contemplation is "street spirituality," gathered in dialogue, it has benefited by responses drawn from workshops and from personal experience during recent years. It has grown more concrete and practical.

Noisy contemplation attempts to put words to people's experiences so they may "own" and celebrate the way in which God's Spirit breathes in the daily experiences of their lives.

To sustain people as loving human beings during the long and arduous work of justice and peacemaking is the dream of noisy contemplation. As world powers expand their arsenals, people of faith show new willingness to confront violence with love and prayer, the weapons of the poor, the armament of Jesus. To do this we need the support of deep prayer.

Experience continues to reinforce the conviction that ordinary people can pray deeply. Jesus prayed throughout a busy, "activist" ministry. He encourages us to do likewise. Jesus engaged in noisy contemplation and so can we.

# Introduction

DEEP PRAYER NEEDS silence and separation from the concerns of ordinary living in order to flourish, doesn't it? To find God we've to put aside our other cares, don't we? Too much activity will burn people out and ruin their religious spirit, won't it? "I never go out of my cell but I return less of a man (sic)," said the medieval writer, Thomas à Kempis, in the *Imitation of Christ*.

These views have ancient roots but grew especially strong in the days when early Christians, judging the Roman world corrupt and dangerous to faith, fled the cities and found God deeply in the desert.

News of their experience brought others to join them. From these communities grew the monastic movement whose serene, silent and ordered finding of God became the norm for all prayer, even that of active people.

Prayer, the "raising of the mind and heart to God," thus was presumed to need surroundings of silence and separation. Only people who followed such a way of life could hope to pray deeply.

*Modern Call to Action*

As long as the world was embattled, it made sense that religious people should try to stay apart and protect faith from a hostile and dangerous world.

Yet, after the Second World War, our world grew populous, urban and noisy. The Second Vatican council, with strong support from Pope John XXIII, encouraged Roman Catholics to abandon their defensive posture and go forth to share the "hopes and joys, the sufferings and sorrows of the people of this earth, especially those who are poor or in any way oppressed."

As people tried to do so, they found that patterns of prayer based upon silence and separation were often swamped by the demands of ministry. Guilt followed over not praying. People feared "activism" and "burnout."

A question arises. Are we being called to give up prayer? Are we summoned to forsake religious experience for the sake of ministry, as St. Paul was willing to forsake salvation if doing so would benefit others? Or can we live an active, noisy, inserted life and still pray deeply?

This book answers the last question with a resounding "YES!" It suggests that the great contemplative tradition is incomplete, developed only for a lifestyle of silence and separation from our noisy existence.

Ahead lies the rapid growth of the complementary tradition, that of contemplative prayer for people who live active, inserted lives. This is the typical pattern of most Christians, the pattern of Jesus' ministry.

This book proposes that deep contemplative prayer is not restricted to a few people with special gifts, but is open to every Christian.

Noisy contemplation seeks to build habits of contemplative praying which can flourish in the ordinary surroundings of our day, including situations of tension and conflict.

These habits of prayer are based upon the experiences of our lives and upon our efforts to live the great commandment. By building contemplative habits throughout our daily lives, we can reach out in prayer to bond with God, with ourselves and with our near and distant neighbors.

By expanding our prayer to embrace all dimensions of the great commandment, praying becomes a way to integrate our lives so that we grow in faith, hope and love in the midst of our active, busy existence.

*How Shall We Proceed?*

Let's begin with stories of people who want to pray. We can then reflect at length on the life, ministry, teaching and examples of praying found in that finest of all models for Christian living – Jesus.

From there we will consider the marks of a simple and achievable spirituality which ordinary people can follow and which builds toward "praying always."

We'll then consider ways to fashion habits of noisy contemplation which embrace all the dimensions of our lives, even reaching out to distant sisters and brothers.

Noisy contemplation welcomes moments apart, the "prayer of perspective." It is also a powerful help for situations of tension and conflict, including the long struggles to bring forth justice upon the earth.

Our goal is to build a life of prayer that can nourish millions of people in the midst of modern living and to celebrate God and God's beloved people: you – me – all of us.

CHARLIE IS A carpenter who is good at his job. The downtown buildings testify to his skills in ways that no one notices. Who sees a smoothly closing door that Charlie trimmed or remembers the forms that cradled the newly poured concrete walls until they were ready to stand on their own?

Charlie, power saw and tools in hand, is at it early today, moving from door to door in the new hotel, checking for a good fit.

His new helper, Mario, like most of the other "gofers," doesn't speak much English. But he's sure willing to do the dirty work if you point out what you want done. Charlie's not sure that these immigrants aren't taking American jobs.

Charlie made a retreat last week with some of the guys from the parish and was truly touched to hear men like himself speak about God, Jesus and love. He was brought up to say his prayers as a kid, but hasn't done much of it in recent years.

How do you pray when you start a noisy job at seven each morning, are dead on your feet when you get home, and ready to fall asleep after dinner? What do you do – contemplate your wife and say your prayers over a beer in front of the TV set?

———————

**Sara** feels the pressure. It's up with the kids in the morning, see them off to school, down toast and a cup of coffee and then grab the bus to work.

It's been two years since she and Mike split up and a year since the divorce. She still isn't free of the nagging guilt that if she'd just been a little more patient with the drinking, the infidelities, the macho spirit, the incessant fighting, maybe he might have changed. Isn't that what Christ was talking about, forgiving the hard things?

But life was awful. Communications broke down. They needed her job and income to stay afloat, but she was the one who wound up with two jobs, one during the day, the other at home, and taking abuse as well.

———————

**Catherine** lives on the sea-swept Atlantic cliff where it juts farthest into the ocean. The view from the great picture window looking down the coast is precisely why she chose this place to live and do her painting.

Whether it's the still waters on a foggy day, the whitecaps in the freshening wind, or the way the pounding surf rides up and crashes over the breakwater in northeast storms, the sea never fails to stir her heart and artist's eye. Her seascapes are starting to find a market.

She sits by the hour watching the ocean exercise against the rocks. The gulls soaring overhead, the sandpipers patrolling the beaches on foot, the ospreys newly returned after near extinction – all have made their way into her works.

Catherine has found it easy to be with God since she moved back near her beloved ocean.

––––––––––

**Joe** sits at the unemployment desk to interview people when they first apply. All types come in during these days of recession: construction workers waiting for a housing revival, teachers ousted by the budget cuts, factory workers cut when the plant went south, sales people dropped when the store closed.

Nowadays you even find a lot of white collar types, nervous, angry, embarrassed, looking guilty about being there.

The cut in the unemployment office staff makes the painful process even more difficult. The lines are longer and the people angrier than ever. They wonder what's gone wrong with their lives. They're worried that no one will want to hire them again and that good days will never return.

Joe likes people, but now he often hates to go to work. The applicants need a focus for their anger. The staff in the unemployment office are "it."

Joe prays about it, but how does saying some prayers help unemployed people or make it easier to deal with them?

––––––––––

**Sister Frances** used to teach, as did all of the sisters in her community. The days flowed in orderly rhythms of prayer, classes and school work.

Religious houses were quiet in those days. The religious habit assured her of respect (even a discount) wherever she went.

How it's changed! The city neighborhood where she lives with three other sisters is hot and raucous in the summer. Racial and ethnic tensions have made people wary.

Sister Frances works with welfare parents, but often feels the suspicion when she's among people who don't know her. Maybe people are right when they say she'd be safer if she wore a habit. Yet many people know her and greet her with warmth and affection.

Prayer isn't easy any more. A stream of people drop by the house and the phone is busy. Cooking, cleaning, shopping and repairs take time. Her rising consciousness of sexism in church ministries and language makes attendance at local parish liturgies painful.

Sister Frances wants to pray. But how does she pray when she's a zombie until morning coffee, busy in ministry all day and she falls into bed too late to get fully rested?

Friends tell her that she should take time off. But the poor people she works with don't take time off and she feels a call to share life with them as fully as possible.

———————

Ken is 16 and near the end of his junior year. Driver's permit in his pocket, he's already been allowed to drive the family car around town on daytime errands. His gang of young men and women who share the school orchestra are a great bunch who enjoy life and each other's company without having to get too serious.

Ken likes church, although he'd never admit it to his friends. Ever since he became an altar server, he's loved the peace and quiet of a visit as well as the ceremonies. He tries to say his prayers each evening, but words don't suffice.

Ken would rather look at the sky, the trees, the birds or even the frogs that they dissect in biology class. The colors of sunset stir his heart with the wonder of God. God seems a lot bigger than any church can contain, but the priests make a big deal of Sunday mass and saying your prayers. There isn't anyone to talk to.

---

**Mary** acknowledges the advancing years. Her husband Tom died four years ago when they were both 75. Life has been lonely, even though her daughter and son-in-law have tried to make her feel at home. The eyes don't see as clearly as they once did and she knows she's getting old. But, all in all, Mary feels pretty good.

It's still a joy to be only a block from the church. She joins several old friends there for Mass in the morning and returns later to say the beads and just sit there with God. "Wouldn't it be nice to pray more deeply?" she has thought, "but of course that's for holy people in the convents and monasteries."

---

**Peggy** is "flat out" at school. The budget cuts have packed her class-room wall-to-wall with kids. The slash in support staff means noisy halls. The teachers have worked without a contract for months, but who needs a strike when unemployed teachers are waiting in the wings? The atmosphere is touchy. Long-time friends are flaring up at each other.

Peggy has been active in church circles, taught religious education classes and was on the parish council. But the pressures at school, the expanded preparation and correcting papers and the tense contract meetings no longer leave much time for church affairs.

Joe is a great support at home, but she doesn't feel very Christian where the school board is concerned. It's as though a lifetime of Catholic education, prayer and going to church is no help in the midst of the present tensions.

***

**Denise & Pat** have been married for 24 years. Their four "children" bracket the teens. Mary, 21, excels in college and worries about a job. Tom, 18, athletic and easygoing, has started college on the work-study plan after months of wondering about whether or not to go. Sue, 12, is the baby of the family, too spoiled, but easy to take. Pete, 15, is the challenge. Unhappy in his brother's shadow, he fights everyone.

The years of financial scrambling have taken a toll that is only starting to ease now that both parents are working and Mary and Tom have jobs to help pay for college.

Denise and Pat know that they don't communicate very well with each other although they get on reasonably well. The years have just seemed to slip by. Friends are urging them to go to marriage counseling.

Toughest of all is the struggle with Pete – to be open and supportive, but firm enough not to let him take the joy out of family life. Everyone is finding it hard to be patient.

***

These individuals are good, caring people of faith. They try to find

God and to be loving. They sense that prayer would be a support for their journey. Some find prayer easy. Others have no such ease.

The pressures of modern living affect everyone, whether it be concern over violence, sex, drugs, AIDS, jobs, or deaths in a distant land, or the many challenges to raising children and to loving one another.

Information technology and computers are saturating the interstices of our lives. The ever-present nagging of the cell phones, the counterpoint of text messaging, e-mail blasts, spam, WiFi coverage, identity theft, drivers talking on their cell phones in heavy traffic, phone cameras, etc. The impact is still in its infancy, but its potential for good is enormous, as responses to natural disasters illustrate. Information technology is here to stay. It is becoming an integral part of the spiritual life.

Modern living is marked with inner and outer noise. Our faith and prayer must adapt to this reality or wither. Forms of prayer must be developed which can flourish in the midst of noise and activity.

To see if these directions reflect the Gospel, let us look at a life filled with activity, pressure and tensions, not unlike our own: the public life and ministry of Jesus.

Since we are called to follow Jesus and to re-express his spirit in our own way, it is vital that we reflect on the way that he lived, ministered and prayed. Perhaps we can live and pray as Jesus did.

## STUDY QUESTIONS FOR CHAPTER 1

*After each chapter we present a study guide for further reflection. These questions are designed to help you become a noisy contemplative.*

Do you think it is possible to pray in the midst of busy lives?

Which story could you identify with as an example of your prayer life? What is your story?

What is your experience of prayer? Where and when do you pray? Is prayer energizing, boring, erratic?

Why do you pray?

As you study noisy contemplation it will be helpful to keep a journal of your experiences. Keep a brief record of what is happening and what insights come to you.

# Jesus: His Life, Ministry and Prayer   2

## Whom Did People Find?

JESUS CAME FORTH from the town of Nazareth. The son of Mary and of Joseph the carpenter, Jesus preached salvation to the people of Israel who, in the midst of a settled way of life in the Law, looked for a Messiah to free them from the Romans and guide their future destiny.

In Jesus, the people found a Jewish man, garbed and living simply, surrounded by a small band of followers, a man who went about "doing good." He proclaimed a challenging way of Jewish living in which love predominated.

The messianic signs seemed to hover about him. The blind saw, the deaf heard, the crippled walked. Prisoners learned of freedom. To the grieving he spoke of joy, and to the poor he proclaimed the Good News of their empowerment and of God's special love for them.

But the signs were cloaked in such ordinary, simple ways of living and teaching that only faith could penetrate the disguise. For people who insisted that their Messiah come in glory, the camouflage was total. He came as a human being and taught in parables.

Yet, the tenor of his teaching was clear and challenging. Followers had to take responsibility for their actions and live a life of love in which observance of the law was but a first step. Gone were the savored dreams of revenge, swept away by love for enemies. Gone was the freedom to love only those who love them.

His disciples were summoned to love even those who did them harm. They were challenged to walk the extra mile and to forgive others, not just seven times, but "seventy seven times."

This life of faith struck even his disciples as beyond human power. Jesus acknowledged that it was, but promised that God's Spirit would make it a light burden and a sweet yoke.

He loved the law and proclaimed it as a guide for Jewish life. But the law was not a fetish, not "my Law, right or wrong." It must be lived with love and compassion.

In countless examples, Jesus urged people to love in ways that transcended what the law could command. Where the law and basic human needs came in conflict, a person should be guided by love and common sense. If an animal could be pulled from a pit on the Sabbath, a crippled person could be healed.

*How Did Jesus Act?*

It was not merely by words that Jesus taught. The way he lived guaranteed his teaching.

Although the ruling class, the Scribes and Pharisees, might feel rejected, he chose to move among the ordinary people and the outcasts of society, sharing their lot, ministering to their needs.

His life taught his disciples to exclude no one from their love. In a land of clans where strangers were avoided, Jesus welcomed the Samaritans, Greeks and a Canaanite woman bold enough to force her way, not only through his disciples, but even through his own initial prejudices.

Jesus reached out to the blind, to lepers, to crippled men and to women in need of healing.

Jesus welcomed children, the lame and the deaf. Where some savored meting out punishment for sinners, Jesus protected the sinners with a dynamic mercy which held up to accusers the mirror of their own sinfulness.

In a society where men did not speak with women in public, not even with their wives, Jesus welcomed women as disciples and friends. He defended them from accusers, talked with them in public, welcomed Mary to sit and learn among his disciples, and appeared first to a woman when he rose from the dead. He sent her as his apostle to inform the disciples that he lived.

*Jesus: A Person of Passionate Caring*

Jesus clearly experienced deep passion – love, anger, frustration, sadness: all of the human emotions.

His love for us is shown throughout the Scriptures by the life he lived and the death he was willing to die on our behalf.

He faced the painful and dangerous rejection by his own neighbors in Nazareth and worked through that to continue his ministry in other parts of Israel (Lk. 4).

Jesus was rejected by most of his own disciples when he spoke of himself as the "bread of life that came down from heaven," a bread that they must eat and drink to have life eternal (Jn. 6). "Because of this, many of his disciples turned back and would not go with him any more" (Jn. 6:66).

Jesus, deeply vulnerable at this moment of rejection, turned and asked the twelve disciples, "And you – would you like to leave also?"

We can feel how touching it was for him to hear Simon Peter say, "To whom would we go? You have the words of eternal life" (Jn. 6:68).

Jesus came back to danger in Jerusalem so that he might respond to Mary and Martha's note, "The man you love is ill" (Jn. 11:4). He met Mary. "At the sight of her tears, Jesus said in great distress, with a sigh that came straight from the heart, 'Where have you laid him?'" They said, "Come and see." Jesus wept (Jn. 11:33-35).

Near the end of his ministry, Jesus felt enormous passion and anger toward the Scribes and Pharisees, whose hostility and opposition had frustrated his ministry and scared away the people.

Throughout the powerful summation of Matthew 23, he castigated the Scribes and Pharisees for their hypocrisy, their use of religion to seek honors and for offering no support for the peoples' religious living. In devastating images he called them "hypocrites," "blind guides" who were exact in trivia but neglected "justice, mercy, good faith," kin of those "who murdered the prophets."

Jesus' deep frustration and anger were cast against a backdrop of contemplative love for Israel which spurred his ministry. "Jerusalem, Jerusalem... How often have I longed to gather all your people, as a hen gathers her chicks under her wings, and you refused" (Mt. 23:27).

Throughout these examples, Jesus seems to have faced conflicts rather than avoid them. He confronted death, the likely outcome of his ministry. He looked straight at his betrayal by Judas and his denial by Peter and the disciples. Far from crippling him, this gaze enabled him to view the future with the gentleness and hope that he displayed at the Last Supper, where his compassion for the timidity and anxieties of his disciples, despite fears of his own imminent death, is striking.

### Noise & Conflict in Jesus' Ministry

When Jesus gathered a band of disciples, crowds began seeking him out to listen and to be healed. Like reporters at a press conference, they competed for his attention. So demanding were the people that some made a hole through the roof of a crowded house to seek healing for a paralyzed man (Lk. 5).

Jesus' public ministry was surrounded by tensions and conflict. His forceful teaching and personal authority challenged people. "Of God," said some; "of Beelzebul," said others (Mt. 5).

When Jesus preached at Nazareth, the initial welcome turned to violent anger when he reminded his listeners that God often sent prophets to people other than those in Israel because prophets are not accepted in their own countries (Lk. 4:24). The people tried to kill him.

Although Jesus preached and acted lovingly, he promised that people would find his ministry controversial. "Do not suppose that I have come to bring peace to the earth: it is not peace I have come to bring but a sword" (Mt. 10:34).

Jesus predicted that his ministry would end in death at the hands of the threatened leaders of Israel, and prophesied that people would persecute his disciples.

He told his disciples that if anyone wanted to follow him, he or she should take up their cross and follow him (Mk. 8:31-38). This way of the cross is not a momentary willingness to suffer a bit for the sake of the Gospel, but a way of living to be taken up "every day."

Jesus implied that such a way of life would be eminently bearable. Indeed, the reward would, paradoxically, be great. He promised that whoever was willing to lose a life for his sake would save it, while those who sought to save their lives would lose them (Lk. 9:23-26).

As Jesus' ministry expanded, the tensions and conflicts mounted. The Pharisees sent people to observe him, to test him, and to discredit him. Failing this, they sought to kill him in order to remove the threat he posed to their authority and control over the people.

For a time, Jesus stayed in the safety of the countryside. But eventually he set his face toward Jerusalem. The disciples feared the danger, yet their hearts were willing. "Let us go, too, and die with him," said Thomas, as Jesus set out for the tomb of Lazarus (Jn. 11:16).

Jesus' prediction of his suffering and death was accurate. He was seized, judged and put to death on the cross. His disciples were scattered and despair settled in their hearts. "Our own hope had been that he would be the one to set Israel free" (Lk. 24:21). When he rose and appeared to the disciples, they were frightened and unbelieving. He called them back to hope. The coming of his Spirit at Pentecost sent them forth to preach the Good News of love.

The same pattern of persecution and conflict followed their ministry. They were hounded, called atheists and forced to live underground, in constant danger of discovery. Many were caught and killed.

Jesus was right. His followers would be persecuted. Much of the killing would be done by people who claimed to do it for God: "... indeed, the hour is coming when anyone who kills you will claim to be serving God" ( Jn. 16:2).

**SUMMARY:** It is clear that the ministry of love which Jesus preached was an arduous, noisy, "activist" ministry, surrounded by the tensions that permeate any group which knows it is under surveillance by hostile authorities who seek to cripple or destroy it.

## How Did Jesus Pray?

How was Jesus able to survive and flourish in the midst of such a noisy, demanding, tense and active way of life not totally unlike our own?

Prayer seems to have played a key role. Let's look at Jesus' prayer. Perhaps we can pray as he did?

## Where & When Did Jesus Pray?

It is clear that Jesus prayed. The Scriptures seem to take for granted that Jesus shared the daily prayers, the Psalms and the rituals of adult, male, lay Israelites. These practices appeared so ordinary to the Gospel writers that they are seldom mentioned.

But Jesus' prayer was more extensive than this. It is clear from the Scriptures that Jesus drew aside to pray. Jesus went into the wilderness, where he fasted and prayed for forty days and forty nights (Mt. 4). Jesus went up a hill to pray (Mk. 6). Jesus prayed alone (Lk. 9:18), an observation that is often repeated by the evangelists.

Sometimes, as at the Transfiguration, Jesus went apart with a few disciples (Lk. 9:28). Sometimes he took the whole group apart so that they could rest from their labors (Mk. 6:31).

Either alone or with his disciples, Jesus clearly welcomed these moments apart, to pray and to rest.

## The Content of Jesus' Prayer

The passages that describe the content of Jesus' prayer are infrequent but illuminating. For example:

* Before raising Lazarus from the dead, Jesus thanked God for hearing him and for helping the people to believe (Jn. 11:41-42).

* When Jesus fasted in the desert (Mt. 4:1-11), he struggled in prayer with the choice of his future ministry. He gazed at the alternatives which the tempter suggested for winning popular acclaim: bread, wonders and joining forces with Satan. Jesus chose the hidden road among simple people.

* The night before he chose twelve disciples Jesus "went out into the hills to pray; and he spent the whole night in prayer to God" (Lk. 6:12-13). It seems likely that he was praying over the choices he would make.

* Jesus was transfigured on Mt. Tabor before the awed gaze of Peter, James and John. Jesus talked with Moses and Elijah "about the way in which he would soon fulfill God's purpose by dying in Jerusalem" (Lk. 9:31).

* Jesus took the same three disciples with him to the Garden of Gethsemani. He asked them to stay nearby while "I go over there to pray" (Mt. 26:36). Jesus faced the dreaded suffering that he intuited lay ahead. In that prayer of agony, he found the courage he needed to go forward with his ministry, even to the Cross.

*Jesus' Teaching About Prayer*

Prayer formed a central core of Jesus' teaching.

When Jesus' disciples asked him to teach them how to pray, he gave them a simple and beautiful example of holding our daily needs up to God (Lk. 11:1-4).

He followed up this teaching with stories of persevering prayer, imaged in the form of "lobbying" God. They should pray like the person who, needing food for an unexpected visitor at night, knocked on an unwilling neighbor's door until the neighbor yielded to end the bother (Lk. 11:5-8).

They should pray like the widow whose persistence wrung from the unjust judge a favorable verdict that neither love of humans nor fear of God could extract (Lk. 18:1-8).

Jesus spoke of humble and hidden prayer, not like the proud, ostentatious Pharisee who prayed on the street corner, but like the publican who quietly acknowledged his sins (Lk. 18:9-14).

Jesus' own praying was a model for the disciples of the kind of prayer that he taught them.

His prayer of praise at the tomb of Lazarus has already been mentioned. More extensive and powerful is John's description of his discourse at the Last Supper, a beautiful mixture of prayer, teaching, reassurance and a promise that his Spirit would keep them safe (Jn. 14:17).

SUMMARY: Although Jesus shared the daily prayers and the rituals of the Jewish people, these appeared so ordinary to the Gospel writers that they are seldom mentioned.

It was his practice of going apart to pray, his teaching about simple ways to pray, his use of prayer to deal with events in his life and his practice of praying aloud in their midst that specially touched the Gospel writers.

### Did Jesus Pray Always?

We now come to a question that is important for setting our expectations of prayer.

Did Jesus pray intermittently, when he had peace and quiet or a chance to get apart, or did he pray steadily throughout his busy ministry?

The question is important because Jesus is our model for Christian living. We need not lay expectations on our own praying that Jesus did not meet. Let's look more directly at his active ministry for further evidence of his prayer.

### Jesus' Encounters With People

Prayer apart was integral to Jesus' ministry. But such moments seem insufficient to explain his actions, including many of his richest encounters with human beings. Jesus often established strong bonds with people even when the time for building relationships was not present. For example: How do we explain Jesus' encounter with the woman reputed a sinner at the house of Simon the Pharisee (Lk. 7)?

Jesus was invited to a dinner to be observed and judged. While they were eating, a woman came in, washed Jesus' feet with her tears, dried them with her hair and anointed them with ointment. Simon secretly scorned Jesus as not much of a prophet to allow such a disreputable woman to touch him. Jesus defended the woman and celebrated her love as more hospitable than that of Simon.

How could Jesus risk his reputation after such a brief, public encounter with the woman? Could it be that Jesus, as many of us treat him, was really "God in human clothing," able to use godly wisdom in order to confound his critics?

If Jesus was simply God in a human disguise, we are protected against having to act as he did. Yet, human beings have been known to act as Jesus did.

---

Archbishop Romero of El Salvador employed, as his liaison with labor unions, a fiery priest whom he was warned not to trust.

The priest did great service but was eventually killed in the midst of popular forces fighting against government troops. Even Romero's closest advisers urged the bishop to distance himself from the priest's funeral.

Romero asked, "Do you think his mother will be there?"

"Of course," they answered.

"Then," said Romero, "I think his bishop should be there, too." He presided at the funeral.

When Jesus, from the midst of a crowd, saw the despised tax collector Zacchaeus in a tree, he invited himself to stay with him (Lk. 19:1-10). The people around Jesus complained bitterly. But Zacchaeus was deeply touched and seems to have been radically changed.

How could Jesus respond this way? Perhaps Jesus drew upon the mysterious beatific vision? Perhaps, when Jesus got up that morning, he reviewed the divine scroll of history and planned the encounters of the day ahead?

Any of these solutions would defend us from having to live and act the way Jesus acted. He was God. We are not!

When Jesus looked on the crowd with compassion (Mt. 14:14) and longed to gather the people of Jerusalem "as a hen gathers her chicks under her wings" (Mt. 23:37-38), what did he see? What vision of love made him ready to condemn the leaders of Israel for their failure to serve the people?

When Jesus met the Samaritan woman at the well (Jn. 4), he was breaking multiple taboos. She was a woman and a Samaritan – a heretic. He talked to her alone in the most public of places, at the well. She was a public sinner, five times married and living with a man not her husband.

Yet, Jesus' meeting with this woman engaged her in the liveliest dialogue of the New Testament.

She went back into the town. By the sheer contagion of her enthusiasm, like a moviegoer infecting others with a desire to see a favorite picture, she drew the people forth to listen to Jesus until they believed on their own.

### HOW COULD JESUS ENCOUNTER THIS WOMAN SO SWIFTLY AND BOND SO DEEPLY?

When Jesus was moving in a crowd one day (Lk. 8:40-48), he suddenly asked, "Who touched me?" He said, "I felt that power had gone out from me." A woman came forward and witnessed her cure from lengthy bleeding.

### WHAT EMPATHY WAS THERE IN JESUS THAT ENABLED HIM TO SENSE HER CURE?

When parents were bringing their children to Jesus, the disciples, perhaps acting like adults who feel that children ruin a religious environment, tried to prevent their coming (Mk. 10:13-16). Jesus rebuked them, called the children to him and proclaimed them a model for all believers.

### WHAT DID HE SEE THAT DIFFERED SO DEEPLY FROM THE DISCIPLES?

When ten lepers, standing afar, called out, other people saw the ravages of the dread disease. Yet, Jesus saw people waiting to be healed. He made them well (Lk. 17:11-19).

### HOW DID JESUS SEE THROUGH THEIR BROKENNESS?

When Jesus was dying, what dynamic enabled him to reach across the distance to the adjoining cross and bond with the penitent thief: "Today you will be with me in paradise" (Lk. 23:43)?

*Jesus' Noisy Contemplation*

In these examples and in many others, Jesus established bonds of love more swiftly than the ordinary dynamics of human relationships make possible. The examples suggest that Jesus approached life in a contemplative way.

Jesus seems to have used his physical senses, his compassion and empathy to contemplate life and the people whom he met. He looked at people, touched them, felt their presence and empathized with their plight with a love that brought deep insight and bonding. This contemplative posture, as the Trappist, Thomas Merton, said, "achieves insight beyond analysis."

Jesus' preaching and parables suggest that he contemplated the earth. Yeast, wheat, figs, fruit trees, oil, salt, light, weather, wine and grapevines are images for faith.

He saw people with a love that cut through past social judgments. He "tuned in" to their present condition and needs. Jesus contemplated people with a love which revealed their hearts to him. He shared his own heart in return.

I believe that this contemplative approach to life was the dynamic which nourished Jesus, the basic way he prayed throughout his days. Sometimes he prayed apart to gain perspective and to rest. But most of his praying was done in the midst of his ministry.

*Jesus prayed constantly and simply by contemplating life as he lived it. Jesus practiced noisy contemplation.*

Such a dynamic would mean that most of Jesus' praying took place by contemplating the people and events of his life at the time he experienced them.

These experiences of contemplative bonding were deeply

nourishing. Far from draining him, the encounters brought him insight into people's hearts and built bonds of love which lasted a lifetime.

*Contemplative Moments in Scripture*

Other people in the Scriptures reveal contemplative insight and bonding in the midst of life. For example:

* The breaking of the bread brought contemplative awareness to the depressed disciples on the road to Emmaus. In a flash of insight, they understood the events of the afternoon and who it was who had walked with them (Lk. 24:31).

* When Jesus said "Mary," the grieving Magdalene suddenly recognized the risen Jesus in the person she had thought to be the gardener. Hearing his voice was the contemplative moment for Mary (Jn. 20:16).

Similar moments of contemplative insight abound: Mary's acceptance of God's invitation to bear Jesus; Elizabeth's grasp of what it meant when the child in her womb leaped for joy at Mary's greeting; Mary's song of liberation in the Magnificat; Simeon and Anna's recognition of the child Jesus in the temple; John the Baptist's encounter with Jesus at the Jordan. The Scriptures are filled with moments in which "insight beyond analysis" came to people whose hearts and senses were open.

To a receptive heart, the world and its people send invitations which resist analysis, but which provide a contemplative base upon which people can build trust, belief and commitment of their lives.

SUMMARY: The example of Jesus and of other people in the Scriptures suggests the possibility and power of noisy contemplation, prayer in which we contemplate life as we live it.

# STUDY QUESTIONS FOR CHAPTER 2

How do you view Jesus? Is he closer to "God in a man's suit," or a human being like us in all but sin?

In what way is your life as noisy as that of Jesus?

Did Jesus pray always or intermittently? Does the book make an adequate case for Jesus' noisy contemplation?

# How Are We Called to Live? 3

O UR CALL IS A SIMPLE ONE. Jesus called us to live the great commandment. "You must love…your God with all your heart, with all your soul, and with all your mind…You must love your neighbor as yourself." (Mt. 22:37-40).

### The Great Commandment

The great commandment is often described as twofold, to love God and to love our neighbor.

In reality, the great commandment has at least *four* dimensions.

* We must love God deeply, both the transcendent God we know only with the eyes of faith and the God who, as Jesus, became a human being and shared all but our sinfulness.

* Our love must be interpersonal. We must love our near neighbors, family, relatives, friends and acquaintances who directly shape our lives and whose lives we sculpt in return.

* Our love must be personal. We must love ourselves so that we can love our neighbors as ourselves.

* Our love must be societal. We must love not only "near neighbors," those who have names and faces, but sisters and brothers who are "distant neighbors," known to us only as citizens of other communities, classes and nations. These people are sisters and brothers equally created by a loving God with an equal right to share the earth.

This love for distant neighbors is the most recent expansion of our consciousness in the great commandment, although continuous with Jesus' love for "Jerusalem" and St. Paul's vision of the mystical body of Christ.

Only in recent years has our expanding consciousness and emphatic church teaching made it clear that every healthy follower of Jesus must embrace the world and share the worldwide struggle for societal love which is justice.

### What Does It Mean?

Our struggle to live our faith often has been a debate over how to live the great commandment.

For centuries, writers emphasized the priority of the "spiritual." Love of God was so primary that the claims of "neighbors" were dwarfed. Activity was believed to dissipate religious energy. Total collapse was likely unless regular prayer guarded against the "world" and its concerns.

To exalt God, theologians stressed our poverty and nothingness.

The days of the Reformation stirred great debates over the relationship of faith and good works, debates which have moderated but not vanished. "Spiritual" people suspect "activists" and expect religious "burnout," while active people judge "spiritual" people wanting in concern for God's people.

Whether it be resurgent Islam, the church's preferential love for the poor in Latin America, prayer in the schools, or the Vatican's views on abortion, stem cell research, or faith-based initiatives, people still debate the place of religion in public policy. How should Christians act out their faith? Should the churches act out their faith in the public realm? Should the churches be involved in politics?

These questions touch the great commandment.

Jesus pointed the way when the lawyer who questioned him asked, "And who is my neighbor?" (Lk. 10:29).

Jesus told the beautiful story of the Good Samaritan, the loving "heretic" who ministered to the broken person after priest and Levite had passed by.

Jesus preached and lived the Good News. The message made sense because he lived out the values and the principles which he taught.

He preached God's love for the poor. He showed special love for the poor "unlovables" of Jewish society: sinners, lepers, heretics, adulterers, tax collectors, foreigners, cripples and the dead.

Jesus preached forgiveness and reconciliation. He forgave sins in the face of authorities who questioned his power to do so. He asked forgiveness for the soldiers nailing him to the cross. He forgave the disciples who deserted him.

Jesus preached meekness and courage. He acted meekly and boldly in the face of Judas' betraying kiss and the soldiers who came to seize him. He proclaimed a love so great that a person might lay down a life for a friend. He laid down his life for us.

Jesus taught that death could not bind those who followed him. His resurrection gave proof of his claims. He promised that his Spirit of love would be with us when we follow him. Countless holy lives bear witness that Jesus has kept his promise. Thus, to live as Jesus did, we must live out the values we proclaim. Words and deeds, values and witness must blend.

*Living the Great Commandment*

Each dimension of our living of the great commandment should reflect this harmony.

To love God, we must spend the time and sharing that human beings need to nurture any relationship. Reading the Scriptures, praying and sharing worship are ordinary and powerful ways of growing in love for God.

To love ourselves, we must reject self-deprecation and accept faith's testimony that we are God's beloved and gifted creatures, made in the image of God.

We must own and exercise our freedom to do good or evil, to be loving or unloving. Out of our freedom to make choices comes a life of liberation.

We must express our love for our near neighbors. Love, affirmation, forgiveness, peacemaking, showing mercy, community building and struggling together in solidarity for the sake of justice must mark our life together.

To love our distant neighbors, we must express a blend of charity for immediate needs and the larger, often conflictual, long-term work for justice that is the chief expression of societal love.

The Roman Synod of 1971 said it powerfully:

> *Action on behalf of justice and participation in the transformation of the world fully appear to us as a constitutive dimension of the preaching of the Gospel, or in other words, of the Church's mission for the redemption of the human race and its liberation from every oppressive situation.*
> — Justice in the World, 1971, Introduction

Pope Paul vi, in his 80th Year "Call to Action" letter of 1971, summoned Christians to act out their faith, not merely in the realm of interpersonal relationships, but in the whole realm of public endeavor, including political and economic life.

SUMMARY: Our call is to follow Jesus, not as slavish imitators of his actions but as people who re-express his spirit in our day. Our guide to this "balanced" way of living is the great commandment. We must love God, love ourselves and love our neighbors near and distant with a love that shows forth in our decisions and deeds.

# STUDY QUESTIONS FOR CHAPTER 3

Do you agree that there are four dimensions to the greatest commandment?

Which do you find easiest?

Which do you find most difficult?

What people do you find most difficult to include in your love?

# Marks of Healthy Prayer   4

I N PREPARING TO BUILD practical habits of noisy contemplation, it will be helpful to remember several tests or guidelines against which we can measure our efforts. These guidelines appear to resonate with the Gospel and with the modern teaching of our faith.

*Healthy prayer is based on our experience*

Prayer is based on the experiences of our lives. God's revelation comes to us through the Scriptures and through the life and tradition of our church, two cornerstones of our faith.

But our primary source of prayer and faith is the experience which each person or community has of the action of God's spirit in our lives. Our trust of this experience rests on the promise Jesus made to us that God's spirit will guide us in understanding what Jesus taught.

Religious institutions have a vital role to play in long-term guidance of religious belief. But each person who chooses to be an adult in faith must trust his or her experience of God. We experience God's grace in daily life. It is here that we make choices to embrace love and to struggle against evil. Our praying must be built upon our daily experience of living.

**EXAMPLE:** A woman taking a workshop lit up at these reflections. "That makes me feel good," she said. "Our family doesn't have much and I'm not very well educated. I just tell God what's happening and give thanks or ask for help."

*Healthy prayer is simple*

Deep prayer, if it is not to be the exclusive domain of a privileged few who are backed by the resources of "religious multinationals," must be so simple that it can be attempted by any person of good will who seeks to follow Jesus.

The more complex the demands of deep prayer, the more specialized and professional the required support staff and the more costly the needed environment of silence and separation, the fewer the people who can consider the journey. Affluent prayer, like affluent pilgrimages, is available only to affluent people.

Simplicity of life is a Christian call that applies, not only to our consumption of the earth's material goods, but also to the resources we devote to nurturing our life of prayer.

Deep prayer for people who want to follow Jesus must be as available as Jesus was to those willing to walk with him. In fact, his promise of the Spirit affirmed that he would be far more available to people of faith than when he trudged the dusty roads of Israel. Such prayer should be able to begin with children and be achievable by people of all educational levels, classes and nations.

Deep prayer must be as simple, yet as deep as the example of prayer which Jesus wove out of daily experiences.

Deep prayer must be as portable as the human being who journeys after Jesus. No "Airstream camper" spirituality, it must be simple enough to be smuggled into prison cells, comfort people who grieve alone and pass between people who have nothing but love to share.

Not for a moment does this emphasis upon simplicity deny the place of professional spiritual directors, of silence, of profound and cultivated skills, of intercultural experiences of prayer, of leisure, learning, serenity or tranquility.

But what this does challenge is the tendency to make such resources seem so essential that ordinary people are kept from the dream of praying deeply when all they have to bring to their following of Jesus are the ordinary, poor, uneducated, tense, anxious and insecure surroundings in which most people exist.

Jesus comes today to the simple and marginal people of the earth, just as he did in Palestine. Modern spirituality must come to grips with that fact.

### Healthy prayer is strong & durable

A key sign of healthy prayer in following Jesus is that it should encourage us in the strong and durable love that Jesus preached. Not for Jesus is a terror-ridden approach to faith which preys upon anxieties and insecurities to manipulate behavior.

Jesus invited people to come as free human beings and to believe that, with his grace, their feelings of fragility, vulnerability, timidity, deep-seated fear and insecurity could be confronted and healed.

Jesus proclaimed a strong and durable faith. To a militant people, he preached peacemaking. To people commanded to avoid adultery, he proclaimed a new limit – to shun even lust in their hearts. To men accustomed to easy dismissal of their wives, he proclaimed permanent commitment. To people who had heard "an eye for an eye and a tooth for a tooth," he blessed a tough, active, non-violent meekness which offered the wicked no resistance, walked an extra mile and loaned possessions with generosity.

Jesus challenged his followers, steeped in separation from and hostility toward other tribes, beliefs and nations, to love not only their neighbors, but to love their enemies and pray for those who persecuted them. To a people for whom wealth and possessions were a sign of God's blessings, he preached poverty and security based on their trust in God.

In the Beatitudes, he celebrated the poor in spirit, the gentle. He lauded those who show mercy and promised comfort to those who mourn. He blessed peacemakers and those who work for justice and are persecuted for their efforts.

To marginal people of ill-repute and supposed little worth, he proclaimed a bold message. "You are the salt of the earth," the "light of the world," "a city built on a hilltop," a "light" that must shine before people (Mt. 5:13-15).

Jesus promised that faith would make them bold when they expected to be most fearful.

And all he promised was the paradox that they would find this way of life a "light burden and a sweet yoke" (Mt. 11:30).

Christ came to raise up saints from sinners, the bold from the timid, the wise from the unlearned and martyrs from the weak. He pledged his spirit of love to guide people willing to risk such a venture.

It is clear that Christ proclaimed a way of life which affirmed that faith can encourage fearful and anxious people to assume burdens, make free choices and follow a demanding way of life typical of strong and durable people.

Thus, any healthy spirituality for today's Christians, especially in these days of struggle for justice, must nurture people in the strength and durability of Jesus' original preaching if it is to be holistic and valid. Spiritualities that encourage fragility, timidity, fear and flight are suspect.

**EXAMPLE:** Some preachers crusade on issues calculated to stir fear and anxiety in their listeners. "Homosexuals! Feminists! Communists! Terrorists!" They prey on people's fears in order to forge social and political alliances. Their appeals are far removed from the strength and boldness preached by Jesus.


*Healthy prayer is deep & loving*

Jesus did not call disciples to follow him in a moderate, prudent, cautious way. Indeed, he called them to a deep love and radical commitment. The invitation from Jesus was to people who could risk everything.

The rich young man, so pious and observant, could not face the totality to which Jesus invited him (Lk. 18:18-23), while the disciples could, even though not sure what lay ahead.

Jesus' call to love invited a total opening of our hearts, not only to those who love us, but even to enemies who persecute and kill us.

Jesus invited people, not to a faith that found zest in a bit of challenge, but to a radical faith that could face failure, even death, and still hope that love would overcome evil and that life would vanquish death.

The Gospel is not a call to socially proper, neatly dressed, politely mannered, law-abiding religious observance. These features may have their place. But they are secondary to Jesus' invitation to become passionate followers, with a love that cannot be tamed by honor or wealth, nor deterred by threats of death. Jesus calls us to a deep and abiding love whose consequences we may not be able to control, manage or plan.

Thus, any spirituality which adequately reflects the Gospel must support Christ's invitation to a deep, passionate, committed love for God, for ourselves and for sisters and brothers near and far.

**EXAMPLE:** One such person was Jean Donovan, a Catholic lay missioner martyred in 1980 in El Salvador. Shortly before her death she wrote to a friend:

> *I love life and I love living. While I feel compassion and care for the people here, I am not up for suicide… Several times I decided to leave. I almost could, except for the children – the poor, bruised victims of this adult lunacy. Who would care for them? Whose heart could be so staunch as to favor the reasonable thing in a sea of their tears and loneliness? Not mine, dear friend, not mine.*
>
> — Letter to a friend, 1980

*Healthy prayer is hospitable*

A key mark of healthy prayer is that it encourages the person who follows Jesus to an ever deepening hospitality.

It seems almost a truism to say that persons who love deeply will act out that love and welcome others into their hearts and lives. Whether the person praying be a busy family member, a single person, a member of a religious order, cloistered or active, the test of hospitality is a test of healthy prayer and the following of Jesus.

Jesus did not encourage us to "look out for #1," or to make our personal fulfillment the pinnacle of our dreams.

Jesus told us that when we give away our lives, we find them. When the grain falls to the earth and dies, it brings forth life a hundredfold. No matter how much such ideas have been abused to manipulate religious and social behavior, the central core remains: when we open our hearts to others and give our love away, we find love.

EXAMPLE: In the 1970s there was a cloistered monastery with much land and few monks. Some poor people asked them to use a little land to raise food for their community. Several monks who were white would not trust the people because they were black. These monks stirred up the affluent people of the countryside to block the monastery from lending any land to the poor people. In order to keep peace in the monastery and in the surrounding community, the abbot refused the request of the poor.

The seemingly deep contemplative prayer of this community was revealed to be flawed. It lacked sufficient hospitality of heart to be able to overcome the racial prejudice of some of its members or to act in the face of their pressure.

How different the decades of hospitality to the poor offered by the houses of the Catholic Worker under the guiding spirit of Dorothy Day. How different the ministry of Mother Teresa and her sisters to the poorest of the dying in India. How different the 1980s welcome of Indo-Chinese refugees extended by so many parishes and families. How different the hospice ministry to those with AIDS. How different the open hearts of many families who adopt children into their love.

For prayer to be mature, it must be hospitable.

### Socially Conscious

Jesus ministered to many individuals in the land of Palestine. But it is clear that his call was societal. He was sent, not just to a few individuals, but to the entire people of Israel. This larger consciousness was a guiding star of his ministry, expressed in the poignant cry of frustration in Matthew 23, "Jerusalem, Jerusalem, how I longed to gather all your children...and you refused."

Jesus sent the disciples forth to preach the Gospel, not just to the people of Israel, but "to all people everywhere."

The most intense call of the modern church re-echoes this mandate. We are to open our hearts to our brothers and sisters throughout the world. It is the call to justice, the call to societal love.

If our prayer is sound, it must empower and nurture such love in the hearts of people who follow Jesus. If "action on behalf of justice and participation in the transformation of the world" is a "constitutive dimension of the preaching of the Gospel," as the 1971 Synod told us, then healthy prayer must support people in this Gospel activity.

Our modern experience with AIDS shows us what happens when we lack a contemplative gaze. When the AIDS virus first appeared in the 1980s, people quickly stereotyped it as a disease of homosexuals. And some church leaders even suggested it was God's punishment for immoral behavior.

It took more than twenty years to understand the scale of the epidemic especially as it has ravaged Africa and for us to become part of the struggle to rein in the AIDS suffering, including our willingness to demand that the drug companies yield some of their profits to make the drug treatments affordable.

Spiritualities which encourage people to focus on "Jesus and me" can nurture for a time. At best, they lack the mature living of the great commandment which summons us to let our near and distant neighbors have an integral place in our hearts. At worst, they lead to spiritual selfishness and religious narcissism.

Without societal consciousness and love, people too easily fall into the trap of a religious faith lived in the semi-private realm of family and friends, a faith which asks no public questions. "Separation of church and state" takes place in our personal religious consciousness. We become uncritical allies of political or economic situations which are at odds with the Gospel.

We live in human society, are shaped by it and shape it in return. We can no more avoid faith choices about public questions than about questions of private and interpersonal morality.

Societal love is not new to Christians. Early disciples spread the Good News through Mediterranean lands. European missionaries, unintended allies of colonialism, set off to convert "the noble savages." U.S. children of the 1920s and 1930s saved their nickels to "buy pagan babies," and listened raptly as missionaries told stories of distant lands and people among whom they ministered. St. Thérèse of Lisieux, the cloistered contemplative, and St. Francis Xavier, the missionary, are both patrons of the missions. Societal consciousness is part of healthy praying.

We must set our face toward society, just as Abraham and Sarah set their face toward the land to which God's promise directed them.

Once we have "set our faces" toward human society, noisy contemplation, especially that in which we contemplatively share the lived experience of others, will deepen our love and strengthen our solidarity of hearts.

### Integrated

When a person sets out to live the great commandment and opens his or her heart to all dimensions of this way of life, an integrated person is growing. Faith values blend with the decisions of our lives. Our actions seek to express our values.

Such a way of life is not without challenge in a world where selfishness is encouraged, greed admired and power worshiped. To follow the Gospel in such an ambience is to be labeled "socially deviant," as was Jesus. Powerful support is needed to walk this Gospel journey.

Noisy contemplation, the prayer of life, can become a dynamic which integrates our experiences, expands our hearts and bonds us in solidarity with sisters and brothers near and far. Such is the practical dream of noisy contemplation.

# STUDY QUESTIONS FOR CHAPTER 4

Discuss the six signs of a healthy spirituality. What do you think of them? How do they agree with or differ from what you have learned in the past? Which dimensions seem most important?

What is your understanding of spirituality now, as compared to your past?

# *Prayer and Contemplation*   5

B EFORE EXPLORING THE DYNAMICS of noisy contemplation, let us reflect upon our background in prayer. Where do we begin? As children we memorized *vocal prayers.* Like old friends, prayers such as the "Lord's Prayer" and the "Hail Mary" bring deep meaning to people who love them.

Vocal prayers such as novenas, the Morning Offering, litanies, ejaculations and other prayers of devotion have long nurtured great and holy people of faith.

In *liturgical prayer,* people gather about the altar to share the Eucharist and to listen to the Word of God.

In worship, the group can become more than a collection of individuals. It can become a community, praying in song, in silence and in ritual.

For many communities of religious, gathering to recite the Divine Office combines vocal and liturgical prayer in a shared, communal setting.

*The Scriptures* are basic to prayer. Pondering God's Word and the story of our salvation stir our devotion and encourage us to follow Jesus. *Spiritual reading* can encourage us in our own faith.

For those seeking to pray more deeply, *meditative prayer* has been the usual starting point. Beginning with reflection upon Scripture or upon some chosen religious theme, the person seeks to ponder more deeply the events described. The person can reflect on the way that this experience speaks to his or her own life, concluding with expressions of love for God and perhaps a resolution for future behavior.

**Contemplative prayer** *is used to describe prayer in which emotions, the affective part of us, come into fuller play. Contemplative prayer is marked by a growing simplicity of intellectual effort, leaving our hearts and our emotions free to penetrate and bond.*

Various stages of contemplative prayer have been marked off over the centuries.

*Acquired contemplation* describes contemplative prayer that persons of good will, responding to the grace of God, can reach on their own efforts. *Simple awareness, prayer of the heart,* the *prayer of simple regard,* are other names which try to describe it. It is to this stage of prayer that noisy contemplation most closely corresponds.

After an extended period in such praying, the person typically passed into a purifying experience of desolation and dryness, named the "dark night of the senses" by spiritual writers.

From there, the person might progress to *infused contemplation,* mystical prayer, where God intervenes more directly. The heights of mystical prayer can lead to deep union with God, such as that reached by St. Teresa of Avila, St. John of the Cross and a few other people specially gifted by God.

*Prayer in Religious Orders*

Contemplative prayer in Europe developed in the monastic communities of the late Middle Ages when Europe grew more stable. The Benedictines powerfully shaped the early movement. Later groups, such as the Carthusians and Cistercians, brought forth their dream of a life totally dedicated to prayer in an ambience of total silence and serenity set deep in the countryside.

Great mystics arose such as Bernard of Clairvaux, Julian of Norwich, Meister Eckhardt, Teresa of Avila and John of the Cross. Contemplative prayer was esteemed and encouraged.

This changed at the time of the Reformation when Protestants and Roman Catholics clashed over the authority of the Church.

Protestants emphasized individual reading of the Scriptures as the primary way to God. Roman Catholics fought back and emphasized the Church as the primary road to salvation and as the principal interpreter of God's Word.

Thus, the Roman Catholic Church discouraged individual contact with the Scriptures at the very time when the new printing presses made the Bible widely available. This separation of Roman Catholics from personal familiarity with the Scriptures only began to be remedied in the late 20th century.

Contemplative prayer also came under suspicion in Roman Catholic circles because it could lead to direct experience of God outside ordinary church channels of interpretation. Such prayer was not forbidden, but came under a cloud of suspicion. Its dangers and illusions were so stressed that few people dared to risk it.

The emerging "active" religious orders of the 16th century (named "active" to distinguish them from the monastic communities who recited the hours of the Divine Office in common) settled into the "safer" channels of vocal and meditative prayer.

This muting of contemplation occurred even for followers of St. Ignatius of Loyola, the founder of the Jesuits, who had encouraged his followers to be "contemplatives in action." Contemplative prayer had arisen in the religious communities, yet religious themselves had grown cautious of it.

### The Prayer of Ordinary People

In the early church, people shared the Eucharist, listened to the Old Testament, the stories of Jesus and letters from disciples. They welcomed people with great hospitality. They cared for one another with a striking charity which attracted people to the community.

After Rome came to terms with Christians in the 4th century, some lay Christians fled to the desert, beginning what would become the monastic movement.

Three key trends were developing in the Church:

* Prayer was becoming a private journey of faith.
* Ministry and decision-making were becoming centralized in the clergy.
* Prayer was becoming professionalized in the emerging religious orders.

Monastic authors wrote so enthusiastically of their experience that their lifestyle and understanding of prayer became the dominant model for all Christian expectations of deep prayer.

At the same time, little attention was being given to the prayers of ordinary people. Their praying centered on participation in liturgies and in reciting vocal prayers.

By the Middle Ages, ordinary people could no longer understand the language of the mass. As Dr. Francine Cardman describes it in her brief but excellent article on spirituality in *The Wind Is Rising* (Quixote Center, 1978), "When direct glimpses of popular spirituality are possible, the picture is of paganism thinly overlaid with Christianity, a mixture of magic and superstition shaped to the circumstances of medieval life."

By the time of the Reformation, devotion to Mary and devotion to saints, although castigated by Protestants, brought warmth and piety and gave ordinary people models for Christian living to whom they might relate with affection. Such devotions were especially welcome during days when vibrant Protestant and Roman Catholic preachers celebrated a harsh and judging God (who was always on their side and who loved to condemn people to hell). Roman Catholic devotion to Mary reached a pinnacle in the 1950s.

The Second Vatican Council (1962–1965) summed up and set in motion several major changes in Roman Catholic life and devotion.

The three key developments are now being reversed:

* Prayer is moving back toward the community.
* Ministry is broadening and becoming decentralized.
* Prayer is expanding beyond the religious orders into the broader faith community.

The liturgical revival, especially the use of the vernacular, has emphasized devotion to Jesus. This has lessened the focus upon Mary and the saints. This shift has also been fostered by the resurgent Roman Catholic attention to the Scriptures.

The last forty years have witnessed a revival of interest in prayer and spirituality. Houses of prayer, prayer groups, spontaneous prayer, charismatic prayer and Rite of Christian Initiation of Adults (RCIA) have touched many lives. Directed retreats, centering prayer, the Liturgy of the Hours and other prayer experiences have sparked a renewed interest. Many people have felt Jesus' saving love in a way that has been new and intense.

The training of a new cadre of spiritual directors, integrating insights from psychology and counseling, has brought expertise and wisdom to support people who pray.

Monastic expectations and patterns have continued to dominate the revival of prayer. But efforts have begun to develop an approach to deep prayer which uses the activity and "noise" of human living as the fuel for habits of deep prayer which are within the reach of ordinary people.

To articulate ways to achieve such prayer is the goal of noisy contemplation.

## STUDY QUESTIONS FOR CHAPTER 5

What prayer forms do you like best? Does one
predominate?

Have you had any contemplative experiences? What
were they like?

# Redescribing Prayer  6
## and Pray-ers

FOR CENTURIES, PRAYER has been defined as "the raising of the mind and heart to God," the simple definition of the catechism. Prayer is rightly affirmed for its power to nurture our relationship to God.

Yet, the measure of Christian salvation is not that of prayer, but the test so vividly described in Matthew 25, that of living the great commandment in deeds which match our commitment to follow Jesus.

When ministry was centralized in the clergy and religious orders, deep prayer was stressed as a support for their ministry. Resources have been lavished to encourage their prayer.

But the Second Vatican Council drew a picture of ministry which is far wider than the service of these professionals. It emphasized St. Paul's vision that each person should serve according to his or her gifts.

The vision has sparked an outpouring of new ministry. Deacons, elders, catechists, delegates of the Word, ministers of the altar, lectors, ministers of the Eucharist, counselors and preachers of the Word mark but the beginning of a vast expansion of people involved in ministry.

This expansion is made doubly necessary in the Roman Catholic community by the aging and diminishing numbers of clergy and religious. But the need for deep prayer is broader than an aid to people who minister in some formal capacity. Deep prayer would be a blessing and support for all who follow Christ.

The experiences which form the basis of such prayer already occur in the lives of countless people. They simply need to be recognized and expanded into regular habits of contemplative praying.

Partners who gaze at each other with love, parents who look fondly at their children, people who face themselves truthfully and take responsibility for their lives and gifts, people who perceive the injustice done to others and struggle to reverse their suffering, these are all people close to the dynamics of noisy contemplation. They experience a bonding in love much like the encounter with God in contemplative praying.

In the personal stories from Chapter 1, Catherine, gazing at the ocean, bonds with it in a way that touches her, just as does Mary sitting alone with God in church.

The experience of Jesus in contemplating God, people, the earth around us and the very events of our lives suggests that the contemplative dynamic can be expanded to embrace all dimensions of living the great commandment.

Thus, we grow more loving when we pray directly to God and when we bond with ourselves and with our neighbors, near and distant. We follow Jesus when we deal lovingly with our own personal existence.

The experiences of our daily lives can become the source of our praying, just as they form the base of our experience of God. Prayer can be a dynamic not only to bond with God directly, but to expand our life in God by bonding in love with the people and events of our whole existence.

Thus prayer can be re-described as *the raising of our minds and hearts to God, to ourselves, to our neighbors near and far and to the world in which we live.*

Such an approach to prayer encourages us to pray throughout our days. Daily living offers a rich source of prayer. Strong, durable, simple, deep, passionate, serene praying which will flourish in the midst of noisy, busy surroundings can develop. We can pray throughout our days.

It is my belief and experience that contemplative praying, so powerful in reaching out to God in a monastic setting of silence and separation, can be equally powerful in bonding with God and with other people in the very midst of our busy, active lives. Jesus prayed this way throughout his active ministry, and so can we!

## Agricultural Images of Change in Prayer

Noisy contemplation's effort to build prayer that is achievable and nourishing for ordinary people is like the changing patterns by which agriculture attempts to grow food for the people of the earth.

Once, farming seemed simple. Subsistence farming was the way that most people lived. But the application of technology and of petroleum-based products in the United States after the Second World War promised an easy end to world hunger by letting us nourish and protect fragile plants. Fertilizer boosted yields. Pesticides, fungicides and herbicides protected crops from bugs, fungi and weeds. Great machines carved the land and harvested the crops.

Destructive results soon followed. Agriculture became technological and centralized. Family farmers were squeezed from their lands. Soaring energy costs, poisoning of the environment, depletion of water reserves, soil erosion and the development of resistant strains of insects forced us to reconsider the dream.

A new dream is emerging. Instead of protecting fragile crops from enemies, farmers now seek strong, durable plants which can resist predators, grow their own fertilizer, use less water and withstand heat, cold and wind.

These developments will mean that people of simple means, rudimentary skills and poor land can grow more food for themselves.

So also with prayer. Noisy contemplation seeks to develop strong and nutritious prayer which ordinary people can grow in the noisy lowlands and hard-scrabble soil of their experiences.

Noisy contemplation is prayer for crabgrass Christians. Crabgrass grows anywhere. Its roots dig deep and bind the earth. It needs little care, is resistant to drought, wind and sun. People can walk all over it and try to kill it. It will grow where there is even a crack in the sidewalk, but can burst forth in powerful growth when conditions are favorable.

Noisy contemplation is deep prayer which grows wherever Christians find love. It can hunker down and find nourishment when the cross is present and rise in powerful growth when love is flourishing.

Noisy contemplation is like growing African violets. Ordinary people love flowers but don't have the time or skills for orchids. The humble African violet has become the ordinary household's orchid. Its many varieties grow with a minimum of care, food, water, light and attention. It thrives on neglect. During dark winter months, it brings copious blossoms to ordinary homes, even those with only a north window on life.

So also with prayer. Noisy contemplation seeks to develop a rich blossoming of prayer among people of few resources save their experiences of ordinary living and their willingness to be open to God's spirit. It is prayer for active city streets, busy families, growing relationships and a view from the fire escape.

# STUDY QUESTIONS FOR CHAPTER 6

What do you think of the broader description of prayer as "the raising of our mind and heart to God, to ourselves, to our neighbors near and far, and to the world in which we live?"

# Noisy Contemplation: 7
## The Tools We Use

This then is our dream, to build a habit of contemplative prayer which can flourish throughout our days. This prayer will enable us to bond with God, with ourselves and with close and distant neighbors. The love and commitment which flows from this prayer will encourage us to express our gifts for ministry and to struggle to bring forth God's reign of justice and love upon the earth.

### Our External Senses

We use our senses to experience the world around us. Our senses are channels to contemplation, able to grasp whole dimensions of reality in an instant. We use our eyes to bond with our world. We can see a child, a sunset, a tree or an aging loved one.

We use our ears to listen to the sounds of the earth. We can hear thunder, the song of a bird, the music of a symphony or the screech of a skidding tire. We can hear words of love or listen to a friend.

We can feel our world through our sense of touch. We feel heat and cold, the firmness of a rock or the soft coat of a rabbit. We can reach out to hug a person in grief. The hug can share feelings and scan the state of a human being in one perceptive moment.

Our senses of smell and taste can savor foods and distinguish among them. We can detect garlic, Chanel No. 5 and a soiled diaper. Even with our eyes closed, we can smell a new day and the aroma of freshly brewed coffee.

## Our Inner Senses

We have inner senses which we can use for contemplation.

Empathy can "tap into" the inner feelings of another person, even when no words are spoken. Compassion can establish solidarity of hearts which takes away loneliness, shares another's suffering, or forges alliances for the struggles of justice. Intuition can leap beyond the apparent evidence to plumb depths of insight.

## Imagination & Memory

Each of us, to varying degrees, can use our experiences to create mental images or a sense of awareness of people or events not physically present to us. We can remember an event from our childhood, recall the face or voice of a loved one or re-experience a treasured moment.

Drawing on our experiences, we can imagine situations not directly known. Using our imagination, we can be present to Jesus at a scene described in the Scriptures, or we can visit a foreign land.

Each of these channels of knowledge and experience can be enhanced by practice and usage. Parents with a baby find themselves able to hear and interpret sounds which others miss. Native Americans, who relied on their senses for survival, were far more sensitive to the earth and its signs than we are. A skilled police observer can drink in the scene of a crime in one swift glance while those of us less skilled would vainly try to memorize details.

Some people possess a special contemplative bent. But each of us can use our inner and outer senses, our imagination and memory to contemplate life. We can hone these skills.

*Introductory Exercises*

Let's practice some introductory exercises, emphasize the importance of building habits of prayer, consider the prayer of perspective and then go on to the development of various dimensions of noisy contemplation.

**1  STIRRING THE SENSES**

Contemplation relies heavily on our senses. We can exercise them to stir new appreciation of their abilities.

*Use your eyes to look about you. What do you see? How do your eyes perceive the world? Note their ability to focus in or to look broadly.*

*Close your eyes and listen to the world around you. What do you hear? Do your ears grow more sensitive as you listen?*

*Feel objects around you and note the different sensations.*
*Where other senses are localized, any part of our body can*
*sense a touch.*

*Try out your sense of smell and your ability to taste. Do you*
*rely on them much?*

*Look at someone near you and discover what your*
*empathetic ability tells you. Do you typically try to "read"*
*the state of other people?*

*Imagine a person who is suffering. Try to be present to him*
*or her. Can you sense the hurt and bond in compassion?*

## 2  PRAYING SCRIPTURE

We approach Scripture to listen to the word of God tell the story of
our salvation. Meditation seeks to understand more clearly the events
described, that is, the way in which Jesus acted, how he appeared to
people and what he taught.

Contemplation lets us be with Jesus, among the disciples, participating in what they might have experienced.

*Try using your imagination to sit among the disciples while*
*Jesus is teaching them. Look at and listen to him.*

### 3 MEMORIES

Recalling the past is an experience in which human beings delight. We love to tell stories that give us a sense of roots and heritage, even when we dwell too long over past hurts.

Contemplation of our memories can nurture us just as it did the ancient Israelites. Only when they remembered, relived and celebrated their Exodus from Egypt did they fully understand the enormous scope of God's love for them, an understanding largely blocked by the scramble for survival while the events were happening.

So also for us. We often understand our lives only long after events have occurred. Contemplating our memories can help us integrate our past, heal bitter memories and bring new openness and confidence for the future.

*Take some loved person or persons, now dead. Use your memory to become present to them. Spend a little time with them and see what happens.*

### 4 DAILY LIFE

Life unfolds in passing minutes. Often it passes without our noticing. Sunsets come and go. Love and friendship are taken for granted until too many years have passed. Children grow up while parents are too busy making a living to spend enough time with them.

Contemplative praying, an open awareness of our hearts toward our experiences, especially toward the people with whom we share life, can transform our daily existence. Such a habit of prayer can call forth beauty and love from what seems daily, ordinary, even ugly.

*Pick some person whom you will meet today, someone you care about. Look at them for a moment in your imagination and then look at them when you first meet them today. See what happens.*

5  **CONTEMPLATING SOCIETY**

A contemplative gaze has few limits. It can travel throughout the world, or even the universe. But we need to practice.

*Pick up your daily newspaper. Pick out a story on the front page. Visit the scene in your imagination and contemplate the scene as the story fills you in on details. See the various people involved and feel what they may be experiencing.*

# STUDY QUESTIONS FOR CHAPTER 7

Experiment with the suggested exercises. Take five minutes for each exercise. Then share back and forth with someone near you.

# *Building Habits of* 8
# *Noisy Contemplation*

C ONTEMPLATIVE BONDING CAN flourish in the midst of the
busyness if we build supportive habits. These habits should
be tailored to our lives, to the rhythms of our days.

A habit automatically triggers a response when stirred by the proper
stimulus. We practice swinging a tennis racket so that in the liveliness
of play, we will take the racket back before the ball arrives and follow
through with our swing.

People who sew or knit or crochet develop habits of touch that
carry them along with proper spacing, tension and choice of stitch,
even when they are chatting with someone else.

We practice typing until our fingers fly and land on the correct
keys (most of the time).

Football players train for years to make reactions so ingrained that
responses become instinctive. They can devote their energies to play-
ing in the heat of the contest.

Musicians practice scales, fingering, tempos, runs, trills and sight
reading until the notes flow effortlessly, leaving time for the shadings
and sonorities that make the music come alive.

Aspiring drivers practice backing up, learning to park, stopping on a hill and braking smoothly, until a skilled driver emerges who reacts automatically when the brake lights flash ahead or a child nears the curb.

Business people develop habits of judgment, an ability to make decisions, plan ahead, assess people who might be specially fitted for their kind of work.

The purpose of habits is not to make life so automatic that we become like the new manufacturing robots which can do the same action accurately, time after time, without fatigue. The purpose of our habits is to free us to savor life.

Habits can be good or bad for us, as the data on smoking remind us. We can grow so addicted to something that the experience demands satisfaction even if we might wish to "kick the habit." Tobacco, alcohol or drugs quickly come to mind, but our ordinary patterns of life and needs for security can become equally addictive.

Good habits can support our living. Addictions can crush our human freedom.

In noisy contemplation, we seek to build habits which support contemplative praying and living in love, not addictions which demand fulfillment to avoid gnawing feelings of guilt at our neglect of prayer. The habits we seek are those which nurture and empower us to live the great commandment.

A general, contemplative posture toward life is our overall goal. However, at any one time, we can focus on and practice separate dimensions of contemplative living.

Thus we can spend a day or week contemplating the world around us. We can change our focus to practice the habit of contemplating people, including ourselves. We can spend time contemplating Jesus in the Scriptures. We can direct our contemplative gaze toward God and spend "quality time" with God.

Like the person who takes course after course in school until an educated and skilled person begins to emerge from the process, our practice of the various dimensions of noisy contemplation adds to our total skill as a praying person.

As with any skill, some people have more ability. Some are more motivated to "stick with it." Some are prodigies.

Yet, as with many basic human skills such as reading, writing and arithmetic, almost everyone can achieve some success if they stay with it.

So little has contemplative prayer been proposed to ordinary people in the faith community that our abilities with such prayer have not been tested, let alone developed.

### Setting Our Face Toward Prayer

The first posture toward contemplative prayer is to want to pray, to want to acquire the habits and skills of prayer.

Duty, compulsion or guilt may nag you to pray more deeply, but they are insufficient. Prayer skills take the time and commitment that only come from wanting to acquire the ability to pray. Praying takes the time and practice of other human skills. You will have to "work at it" if you are to succeed. But noisy contemplation, praying life as we live it, is eminently worth the effort.

We have a powerful promise to support us. Jesus promised us the Spirit. He encouraged us to be simple and persevering in prayer. He pledged that God would hear our prayers and respond. God wants us to succeed at prayer.

Contemplative prayer is a way of growing in love for God, for ourselves and for one another. Jesus did not set us up for chronic failure, but for success in prayer, that is, to grow in love. "What parent among you would hand your children a stone when they asked for bread? Or hand them a snake instead of a fish? ... If you ... know how to give your children what is good, how much more will God give the Holy Spirit to those who ask (Lk. 11:11-13).

Brought up on religious teaching that failure to pray is a fault to be confessed, we often approach prayer as a duty, in which only failure to reach the ideal is likely.

It is important to lay aside any failure-oriented approach to prayer. Instead, like a person learning to macrame, play an instrument, throw a pot, change a diaper, write a computer program, drive a nail, speak a new language, we need to celebrate the early gains as pledges of future growth. The modest successes buoy us to try again until the skill begins to blossom and guides our efforts.

*Starting Out*

We can begin with early morning habits. The "Morning Offering," which so many of us have used to begin our day, can easily remind us to open our hearts and senses to contemplate life during the day ahead. We can ask the grace to greet the day with contemplative eyes.

The actions we repeat every day are an excellent place to build habits of contemplation. A look out the window toward sunrise or a glance toward the sunset can be reminders to keep our eyes open to the created world around us.

A loving glance at a family member or at our rumpled selves in the mirror can set in motion our habit of welcoming people during the day.

For the many people who drive to and from work alone, who walk a bit or who travel alone on public transportation, such repeated actions offer time alone to build habits of contemplating people, nature or God. When a habit such as praying on the journey has matured, merely initiating the journey can call us to prayer.

Parents can build the habit of contemplating their children when they first see them in the morning and send them off to school. Teachers can build a habit of contemplating the members of their class when they first gather in the morning. The habit can be refreshed with the beginning of each new encounter during the day until it grows more habitual and is repeated during classes.

People who work in stores or factories can look about at the people when they enter their place of work, building a habit which encourages them to be open to the people with whom they work during the day.

Such habits of beginning our days and actions with contemplation are precious indeed. They initiate prayer that can expand to fill the day.

Some days will find our hearts open. On those days contemplation may seem easy and extended, like a day of singing when our voices are smooth and melodic.

Other days may be full of dryness, resistance, awkwardness and hardness of heart, days when not a shred of concern stirs except hostility. It is like trying to sing with a case of bronchitis.

Every person learning a new skill experiences days when nothing goes right. It is part of being a human being and knowing the rhythms of our lives. But reminding ourselves to be open, even during such days, can sometimes change the direction of the day and encourage us to love.

St. Ignatius Loyola, the founder of the Jesuits, encouraged Jesuits to look into their hearts twice a day to review briefly how the day was going, to remind themselves of their call to follow Jesus and to encourage themselves to be loving in the hours ahead.

Such a moment of review is precious, especially if made a regular practice. Natural times fall near lunch and in the evening, perhaps just before falling asleep.

Like the time of thanksgiving after the Eucharist, such moments of brief reflection can remind us to give thanks for the blessings of life which have come to us. We will fix events in our memories before they slip away. Remembering the blessings of God's love fosters hope for life ahead.

# STUDY QUESTIONS FOR CHAPTER 8

Do you have some highly developed skills? How did you acquire them? What does this say about praying?

Do you want to pray more deeply? If so, why?

# Prayer Apart: The Prayer of  9
## Perspective

WHEREAS ORDINARY APPROACHES to prayer begin with time apart from life, noisy contemplation starts in the middle of life. In no way does it reject the value of quiet time apart, but its emphasis is upon developing prayer that can flourish throughout our active days.

It treasures time apart from ordinary life to gain perspective. It also celebrates the prayer of perspective that can flow from prayer in the midst of life.

### Prayer of Perspective in Jesus' Life

As we noted before, Jesus lived an active ministry in which people made constant demands upon him, even when his own zeal allowed a "breather." The tensions that surrounded his ministry took their toll on Jesus and the disciples.

Jesus, like every other human being, sought ways to relieve the pressures, conflicts and anxieties, as well as to regenerate his own energies and those of the disciples after periods of intense ministry.

Jesus went apart to pray, either to be alone or to spend some time with the disciples. The Scriptures frequently mention this. For example, he went to a lonely place (Mk. 1:35) to be alone (Lk. 9:18), away with his disciples to rest (Mk. 6:31), up a hill to pray (Mt. 14:23). He spent the night in prayer (Lk. 6:12).

In the midst of his busy life, Jesus often sought to get away from the cities, the crowds, the busyness and the pressures of people's incessant demand of his ministry.

Although whole lives and patterns of prayer have been built upon the description of Jesus' habit of praying apart, there is no evidence that Jesus prayed apart each day, or even on most days. His going apart is striking enough to be noticeable by the writers who, in their economy of description, focus on events that set Jesus in relief to the expectations of a teacher in the Jewish culture.

It does not seem possible to draw from the life of Jesus any patterns of prayer similar to the hour of daily mental prayer or to the structured ambience of monasteries.

Monastic prayer and its way of life are cultural forms that arose later. They came from a sense of Christian call to a life-style in which the patterns of prayer and the environment which supported them bore witness in the fruit of holy lives.

What the pattern of Jesus' life does reveal is that in active, busy lives, it is a blessing to gain sufficient psychic or physical distance from our ordinary living so that we can gain perspective.

Let's consider the place and importance of the prayer of perspective in our lives.

*Prayer of Perspective in Our Lives*

When an artist sets out to paint a large picture, the vast bulk of time and energy will be spent up close to the canvas or wall, putting paint on the surface.

But the artist regularly needs to step back and check the perspective and proportions of the work. From this vantage point, adjustments can be made and new insights developed for the next stage of painting.

Like the artist, we spend the bulk of our time up close to the canvas of our lives, painting in the myriad thoughts and events of our ordinary day.

But like the artist, we need to step back from time to time to gain perspective. Jesus' example encourages us to do this.

When we can manage it, extended time apart for prayer and reflection is a treasure. Without the pressures even of ordinary vacation travel, such days can give relief that sends us home refreshed and relaxed, perhaps with a larger view of our existence.

Such time apart puts in perspective the "daily" dimensions of our lives that can overwhelm us. An experience such as a retreat or vacation can have an impact that lasts for months.

But for most people, the demands of families, work and limited finances put restrictions on extended time apart.

If the prayer of perspective is to be a regular part of noisy contemplation, we must develop such moments of perspective in our daily living.

*Prayer of Perspective in Daily Living*

Active people often develop patterns of aloneness and apartness on a daily basis. Countless joggers pass through busy streets. They keep fit and enjoy a daily dose of solitude. They illustrate one way to get distance from life, that is, to separate themselves physically from their regular surroundings.

A second method is that of psychic separation. Portable earphones can surround us with a world of music. We lose ourselves in a good book. We use the movies to escape our ordinary existence, at least for a few hours. A party or a wedding punctuates our ordinary days with gatherings that are special.

In prayer, many people seek time and space in the day to be alone. Early morning, before the world stirs, is a time preferred by many. For parents, the evening silence is special after the children have gone to bed. It is wisdom that we were encouraged to say our morning and evening prayers.

*Sandwich Praying: Cumulative Habits*

Yet, some of the most available and affordable moments for the prayer of perspective depend upon building contemplative habits in the midst of our lives. Instead of seeking blocks of time to be alone, we can convert many small moments of our day into cumulative habits of prayer.

A habit attached to walking can put us in God's presence, or connect us with someone dear to us at moments throughout our day when we move from one place or task to the next.

Such a habit can be pursued by a farmer or gardener walking across the land, a homemaker moving about the house, a worker shifting location in a warehouse, a teacher passing between classes, a nurse or doctor moving about the hospital, a worker waiting for the next piece on an assembly line.

A habit of contemplation attached to driving or riding can transform commuting into a time for prayer and perspective that, in addition to nourishing prayer, may also assuage the frustrations of commuter travel. (Try contemplating people in adjacent cars during a traffic tie-up!)

We can use these moments, either to be present to God or to contemplate the people and events of our lives.

As Jesus did, we can seek out special moments of apartness when we face major challenges in our lives. When dealing with conflicts or making major decisions, we will benefit from special time apart.

But, like Jesus, we can look forward to finding the bulk of our contemplation, including the prayer of perspective, in the midst of the lives and relationships of our daily living.

*How Can You Tell if It's Contemplation?*

*Slowly!* Authentic prayer will slowly unfold the marks of the Gospel, the marks of God's Spirit.

The real test of contemplation is the impact it has upon our lives. Such an impact can be tested only over a period of time as we trace the tempo and direction of our lives. "By their fruits ye shall know them" is an old truism with perennial validity for praying.

One caution: when reviewing your life do not compare yourself with other people. Your norm of comparison is with the way you have lived in the past. Against that background, seek signs of growth.

Let us now look at some of the various dimensions of life in which noisy contemplation can grow and flourish.

# STUDY QUESTIONS FOR CHAPTER 9

Do you need quiet time for prayer?

Are there moments during your day when you could
build a time for perspective in the middle of your living?

# Contemplating   10
## the Earth and Civilization

### Contemplatives of the Earth

T HE SIMPLEST EXPERIENCE of contemplation for many people
is the experience of contemplating, gazing at, listening to and
bonding with the earth around us. Children, typically, are
fascinated with nature, responding with their persistent, "Why?"

But adults often stop observing and bonding with nature, passing on to other, "more important" concerns. And so the base of our
wonder grows dim.

We forget to look for rainbows when the rain clouds part near
sunset. We get up too late to watch the dawn. We forget to gaze at
the stars and to recall the vast light's journey to reach our eyes. We
take the water for granted and wish the rain would go away. We stop
bending low enough to witness the toiling ant. We lose our wonder
for growing plants and the mysteries by which the seed falls to the
earth and brings forth grain a hundredfold.

On city streets, we pass unseeing as the crabgrass squeezes through
cracks in the pavement. We hurry past the myriad shadows of fire
escapes or bannisters. Soaring buildings or bridges stir no wonder
in our hearts, either in themselves, or as expressions of human

imagination. We ignore the countless people, our sisters and brothers, who flow past us on the sidewalks.

To refresh our childhood sense of wonder in nature, it is necessary only to begin anew, to build upon our years of early experience. In the beginning, if we are rusty and out of practice, we shall have to remind ourselves constantly to open our eyes, our ears and our hearts to what we see.

But so powerful is the call of earth's beauty that a reminded heart will find the experience hard to resist. Invitations to wonder lie all around us.

Whether it be the cloud formations, the shifting weather, the snowflakes with their infinite geometries, the rumble of the thunder, the flash of the lightning, the pounding of the ocean waves in a storm or the gentle swells on a calm summer day, nature's experiences lie all around us.

Thus, opportunities for prayer can occur throughout our lives as the habit of contemplating nature grows within us.

A quick glance at sunset or sunrise on a busy day can bond us with nature, even if no extended moments are available, just as a parent can bond with a child in a swift glance.

To dig the earth, plant seeds and watch them mature with the wind, the sun and the rain until a harvest is ready, is a deep and abiding mystery of God's love for us.

People who become "contemplatives of the earth," such as Catherine at the seashore, people who garden and farm, young people like Ken who love the outdoors, people who reverence the earth and work to preserve it, know well that the forces of nature, the rhythms of the seasons and all growing things confirm the ancient writer, "The earth reveals the glory of God."

As noted before, Jesus contemplated the earth and used examples from nature to illustrate his teaching.

Our prayer of the earth is an expansive prayer, as wonder always is. It brings a sense of health, of human "rootedness" which is God's special gift to people who love and reverence the earth.

## Contemplatives of Civilization

Not only natural phenomena can stir contemplation, but God's glory can shine from the works of human civilization.

Just as the disciples of Jesus looked with awe on the beauty of the Temple of Herod (Lk. 21:5-6), our hearts can be stirred by human civilization.

An airplane passing overhead, a ship sailing the sea, a skyscraper or church steeple soaring toward the sky can stir contemplative wonder. The art of politics and human laws, the systems by which people market and share the earth's resources, when just, can stir our hearts with wonder at God's creation of human beings.

The scientist exploring the laws of nature or adapting materials and plants to serve human life can know a vision of beauty undreamed by those who stereotype scientists as mechanical people.

Artists hold a special place as contemplatives of the earth and of civilization. Whether with words, dance, song, ritual, images or materials, they seek to express their contemplative imagination in ways that can be shared with others.

But most of the contemplation, both of nature and of civilization, is to be done by people like kids who shriek with glee at the sight of their first pollywog and adults who still watch jets soar overhead and who smile at children. Contemplation is for ordinary people.

# STUDY QUESTIONS FOR CHAPTER 10

In the course of a day, what dimensions of nature
do you notice?

What dimensions of civilization?

Where in your life could you build habits of
contemplating the earth and of contemplating
human creations?

# Contemplating People   11

THE SECTION ON the prayer of Jesus proposed that the ordinary, pervasive prayer of Jesus throughout his active ministry was the contemplation of the people he encountered while he ministered.

His contemplative heart reached out to poor, broken, sinful, sick and marginal people to welcome them to new life.

Jesus contemplated people as he met them and bonded with people when there was not time to build ordinary relationships. His eyes invited women and men to follow him.

In a similar dynamic, the Spirit of Jesus reaches out to us in our day, and with a grace-filled touch of love and welcome, invites us to contemplate God's beloved people.

The contemplation of people is pivotal to noisy contemplation. The goal of this prayer is to build habits whereby we approach people with open hearts, and with our senses, inner and outer, alert and welcoming.

Contemplation of people seeks an openness to our "neighbor" which invites a response of love and trust. It adds new dimensions to existing love, invites concern where no previous ties existed and can restore love that has been broken.

If we learn to contemplate people, we will live more fully as followers of Jesus.

### Praying People We Care About

A good place to begin is to contemplate people who already hold a special place in our hearts, family members, spouses, children and cherished friends.

Contemplation of cherished people is usually not a new experience. But we may never have thought of it as contemplative praying, nor realized that it can be developed into a habitual, abiding way to pray.

### Parents & Children

Contemplation is one of the easy habits and great joys of new parents. It is a habit that is critical for the baby's survival. Signs and sounds must be interpreted to know when to feed, when distress is present and when it is all right for parents to relax. Parental senses grow unusually sensitive to small children such that they register a baby's needs even while the parents sleep.

As children grow more self-sufficient, parents rightly pay less attention. The intense, early habit of contemplation begins to erode. Parents now rely on the child to make known his or her needs. Only an unaccustomed scream, strange sound or sudden silence becomes an instant concern.

By teenage years, the child has become such a regular presence in the house that parents often fail to "see" or "hear" this emerging person.

In the midst of conflicts, parents and teenagers often turn anti-contemplative. They lay harsh judgments on each other or stop communicating.

Far different is the experience of parents who keep alive a gentle and regular habit of contemplating their children. They have made the transition from the intense alertness of early years to a more conscious and cultivated habit of daily seeing and opening their hearts to their children.

The habit will often suggest creative ways whereby parents can affirm and celebrate the person they see. Such affirmation, especially if it comes at moments when young people are themselves most unlovable, is one of the greatest gifts that parents or adult family members can offer to young people whose lives are so often filled with adult litanies of "do's and don'ts."

Such a habit, cultivated during the growing years, is the ideal backdrop against which to keep perspective when teenage children begin their intense quest for self-identity.

*Welcome for People Who Love*

When two people first fall in love, contemplation plays a large, unforced role. They delight in looking at each other. They spend welcome hours listening and sharing life.

Yet the "glow" commonly fades with passing years. Routine takes over. Physical presence replaces contemplative openness. People know each other so well that they no longer see or hear the other with close attention.

Family members develop such routine relationships that even fond interactions occur without reflection. Friends lose the attentiveness of early days.

As family members grow old and mental faculties decline, families often avert their gaze, fearing to face the approach of death and the reminders of their own mortality. In a nation which glorifies youthfulness, aging brings stresses that challenge our love.

There is no habit of contemplation more easily built and nourished than that of seeing, looking directly at the person you love when you first enter each other's presence.

This situation is so common, so often repeated and applies so easily to other relationships in our life that it takes a primary place in building habits of noisy contemplation.

Married people can re-initiate the simple habit of looking at each other whenever they first enter the same room or space together. A meeting of eyes, "across a crowded room," can bring warmth and communication when the day is too peopled for private sharing.

By learning to contemplate each other on a regular basis, people will keep fresher the memory of their life together and extend invitations to share their future. Partners like Denise and Pat may find that such contemplation offers a first step to renew communication and, once again, to express their love in creative ways.

Charlie, the carpenter, might well contemplate his wife over a beer when he returns home. Contemplation can flow as freely from tired bodies as from rested ones.

Either partner can build the habit in his or her own life. They simply begin "seeing" the other person when she or he is first present. The moment needs no elaboration save that of an open heart. To greet another person with love is a contemplative moment that speaks with its own eloquence. Love is contagious.

The purpose of the initial greeting is to build a habit that can be easily triggered no matter how busy our days. As the habit grows, we do not have to remind ourselves to extend a welcome. The very entrance into the other person's presence lifts our eyes and heart in a contemplative greeting.

A habit of contemplative welcome is a special joy for people when they build the habit together. Denise and Pat would benefit greatly, especially if they launched the habit with a reinforcing experience such as Marriage Encounter.

People who habitually greet each other contemplatively will find themselves reaching out to each other in creative ways that build sharing, love and sensitivity throughout their times together, even when the moments are far too busy for any but momentary interactions.

Husbands and wives who acquire this habit will quickly know when they need reconciliation. To contemplative eyes, our instincts to avert our eyes and refuse our presence can signal tensions even before other signs suggest something is amiss.

### Friends & Family

Friends can build the same simple habits of contemplating each other, especially when first they meet. It takes not a moment longer to contemplate a friend than it does to enter each other's presence.

If we build a habit of contemplating people, then as members of our family grow old, that loving gaze will keep fresh our awareness of the life we have shared, the person they remain and the person they are becoming. The boldness and empathy so typical of contemplation may well help us adapt gracefully to our own aging.


*People We Do Not Know*

As noted, Jesus often encountered people whom he seems not to have met previously. Many of the deepest and liveliest verses of the *New Testament* describe these moments. The Samaritan woman at the well, the Canaanite woman, Zacchaeus, the woman at the house of Simon the Pharisee, the widow of Naim, the centurion, Bartimaeus the blind man and the man born blind – these and other stories describe Jesus meeting people whom he'd never seen before.

Jesus' openness to people obviously amazed his disciples (including the biblical writers) in a nation where distrust of outsiders and strangers reflected the long struggle to protect their fragile people and land.

Jesus' bold welcome to people set a tone for Christian ministry. He pointed the way for "breakthrough" hospitality, such as the decision of Acts: 15 to welcome Gentiles into the community without requiring them to be circumcised and keep the law of Moses. This hospitality, so reflective of Jesus, extended a hand of greeting to the entire Gentile world.

Jesus' special love for sinners and his welcome of strangers and the outcasts of society into the community played a pivotal role in the growth of the early church.

For us, whether raised on a small town's suspicion of strangers, or possessed of the avoidance mechanisms common to suburbs or cities, contemplating new people seems almost dangerous, liable to give people "the wrong idea."

In our culture, women are expected to ignore strange men, while men who make friendly gestures toward unknown women face instant suspicion. Overtures of men and women toward strangers of their own gender face similar cultural barriers. Most extreme might be our behavior on city subways or on elevator rides. All abide by a tacit agreement never to look directly at another person.

Contemplation of strangers begins with full awareness of these cultural barriers. We may well start contemplating people covertly, casting an occasional glance, or observing them with our peripheral vision, a posture with which most of us are adept.

Slowly we can retrain ourselves to see strangers with the eyes of a faith that reminds us of the love God has for them and of the gifts with which they are endowed.

The practice is not to be confused with the time-honored effort to see Christ in others. We are not trying to see Christ in others (a practice which Jesus seems not to have pursued). We are trying to see the other people for themselves, the approach that Jesus used.

We will often find that when we contemplate other people, we do experience Christ's presence. That people, seen with the eyes of faith, reveal the glory of God should come as no surprise.

Eventually, or even sooner, we might risk some changes in our behavior. We might offer a smile or nod of greeting on a morning street, a welcoming glance in a store, or a new friendliness toward a never-before-acknowledged neighbor. Perhaps the habit of contemplating and welcoming strangers might prove infectious.

This welcome of strangers, which so deeply marked the early church, is needed in our present churches. We often fail to acknowledge others around us, even after years of sharing worship. Recall the continuing struggle to encourage Roman Catholics to exchange a real greeting of "peace," to look at one another, not with trapped eyes, but with welcome and with mutual solidarity in our shared faith.

But wouldn't our encounters with new people overload our already pressured lives?

Hardly! We always retain the power to close ourselves off when we wish. Yet, when we contemplate others we will often discover that the experience of seeing other people and celebrating our mutual life, even for a fleeting moment, adds a warmth and faith that nourishes, not diminishes, our lives.

Such a habit of prayer can reflect the empathy and compassion of Jesus.


## Contemplating People Where We Work

Family surroundings are a key location in which to build habits of contemplating people. We feel special motivation to love our families and friends. People whose work focuses on caring for children, home and family will find this a major expression of their praying.

But Jesus told us not to limit our love to those who love us.

For the many of us who work outside our homes, contemplating people in our workplaces, where we spend a large proportion of our waking hours, is a neglected dimension of prayer with great power for bonding and growth.

For people in the helping professions, medical people, counselors, religious and clergy, teachers, such prayer can transform their workplace from a series of "tasks" into a place of faith, a space to encounter the spirit of God alive in people.

Nurses and doctors who contemplate the people whom they treat will find a compassion that, far from diminishing their professionalism, will enhance their understanding of the patient while it nourishes the medical person as a caring human being.

Many patients give witness that empathy from a doctor or nurse complements or at times surpasses the healing brought about by their technical expertise.

Teachers are called to love their students. Yet teachers, who in early days reveled in their students, grow protective of their own energy. Contemplation of their students can bring nourishment.

How do they contemplate students? Can contemplation occur in the midst of teaching?

Teachers often affirm that while teaching they suddenly know something about a student before them – an insight that pain or fear are present or that something good has happened. Follow-up after class reveals their insight to be accurate.

They have had a contemplative experience, an insight communicated through open senses and a compassionate heart that is able to "tune in," to resonate with the experience of the student. Noisy contemplation seeks to make such openness and bonding habitual.

It takes no longer to contemplate students, that is, to see them with an open gaze, than it does to glance their way or to look at a wall. Since the contemplative experience is based on wonder and openness to human beings who bear the image of God, it can be a loving experience, even when we enter into the pain of another or engage in conflict with them.

Such a habit usually begins with a reminder before class to look at the students and be open to them. Frequent renewal of the practice during the day leads us toward habitual openness. When teachers complement this practice by contemplating and praying to love their students outside of class, the circle of contemplative love is complete.

Teachers who cultivate the art of contemplating their students may discover new insights which help their teaching. At a minimum, it will help them love their students and nourish both teacher and students as human beings.

People who work in manufacturing jobs or offices face challenging workplaces. The tasks may grow so repetitive that they put their minds in neutral in order to deal with the boredom. Human contact may be limited to coffee breaks and lunch.

Yet, God calls us to love the people with whom we work. A habit of noisy contemplation sustained by occasional glances at our coworkers can weave moments of prayer throughout the day.

The job-related examples can be multiplied. Priests can contemplate the people whose confessions they hear, or the people to whom they preach. Bus drivers can contemplate the people who board and depart. Store clerks can contemplate their customers. People, such as Joe in the unemployment office, can contemplate the people who approach his desk. Such prayer can bring love and understanding to daily life and work.

## Contemplating a Broken Love

A key challenge for people who contemplate others is our willingness to behold people whom we do not like, people to whom we have an aversion, or people with whom we once shared love or friendship, but between whom conflict and separation have intervened.

If our praying flows from the Gospel, then it must help us deal, not only with people who love us, but even with "enemies" and people who persecute us (Mt. 5). Such prayer must empower us to face Christ's challenge to forgive one another.

### IN COUPLES

When two people who share life come in conflict with each other, they typically adopt anti-contemplative behavior. They turn away, stop listening, refuse to talk, stiffen their hearts and hold the struggle before the eyes of their imagination.

In their hearts they go round and round, reliving the argument or hurt until the incident deepens and becomes etched. As an astronomer once said, "The moon is the size of an orange held at arm's length." So, also, a hurt held closely can block or warp our perspective.

These anti-contemplative actions have good reasons underlying them. When conflict sums up unrelieved tensions between people, we often prefer to keep the feelings alive. We want time to savor and indulge hurt feelings and time to punish the other person with our rejection.

An anti-contemplative posture helps fan hurt feelings. But if we have a fight with someone we love and turn and look at them, unless we harden our hearts, it is hard to prevent a timid smile or a wry glance from extending an invitation to bridge the separation.

At such times we are like Houdini, the magician who had terrible fights with his wife. He would storm out of the house. When he returned after quieting down, he would open the front door and throw his hat into the house. If his wife did not throw it back out, he knew it was safe to enter and be reconciled.

### IN RELIGION AND POLITICS

Religious and political institutions can be anti-contemplative. They shun dissenters and marginalize people whose behavior they object to. Societies often revel in labeling people "bad," so that "good people" can be reassured of their virtue.

They behave like the Pharisee in the Gospel story who was delighted, not because he was a good person, but because he was not a sinner like that "publican" (Lk. 18:11). Their actions are often phrased in concern for a greater good. "It is better for one person to die for the people, than for the whole nation to be destroyed," said Caiaphas of Jesus (Jn. 11:50).

The anti-contemplative blindness that prejudice induces in the eye of the beholder was fostered by the Reagan Administration's 1980s claim that tiny Nicaragua was a threat to the United States, or the Vatican's fear and hostility toward generous Catholic women who offer their gifts for full ministry among God's people, or the blindness of the George W. Bush Administration and its claims that Iraq had weapons of mass destruction, had assisted the destruction of 9/11, was cooperating with al-Qaeda and that Iraqis would welcome U.S. troops if we invaded.

Contemplation can heal and reconcile institutions and nations, as well as people. When nations, long-time enemies, begin to let themselves re-experience each other, reconciliation becomes possible. Witness the U.S.-Chinese table tennis matches which were the initial gesture to bridge decades of hostility.

Similarly, we, Christians of the United States, are called by our faith to love our sisters and brothers of the former Soviet Union, Cuba and China, even though we were taught to hate communism. If we can experience these people, whom we may have stereotyped as "commies," we can replace our prejudices with love.

Lacking resources for such travel, we must use our imagination to contemplate sisters and brothers whose dreams and hopes, fears and anxieties are similar to our own. In the light of a faith that reminds us of God's equal love for each of us, it is hard to keep hatred in our hearts.

### BETWEEN PARENTS AND CHILDREN

When parents in conflict with their children can bring themselves to simply gaze at their children, not with judgments and censure, but with open eyes, the experience can heal and put in perspective the conflicts of the growing years.

**EXAMPLE:** At a workshop on noisy contemplation the people went home with an assignment to contemplate someone they love but with whom they are in conflict. The next day as we shared stories, a man told this one:

On the way home he had resolved to contemplate his 14-year-old daughter, the oldest of his four children and his favorite. For years they had been close, but the last two had been "hell" as they fought and hurt each other.

The whole family sat down at table, the father at one end, the mother at the other, with children on either side. His daughter sat as far away as possible, never looking at him.

"After the food was served, I decided to try to contemplate her," he said. "I lifted a forkful of mashed potatoes to hide behind and I looked down the table at her. Her head was down. Suddenly it hit me like a ton of bricks! I realized that she was a really good kid, so like me that we clash. She wants to be independent and I don't want her to get hurt.

"I realized that for two years I haven't simply looked at her with love. I've judged her, criticized her and complained about her, but never just looked at her and loved her.

"I also realized that during these two years I haven't said a single affirming word to her. I decided to do something about that. At the end of the meal, when we started to get up together, I rose quickly before she stood up, moved down to her end, leaned down and whispered, 'You're a really neat kid.'

"She jumped up, burst into tears, ran to her room, slammed the door and didn't come out the rest of the evening, nor have I seen her this morning."

He looked around our misty-eyed group and said, "I don't know what's happened, but its different now." Then he asked, "Is this what you mean by noisy contemplation?"

# STUDY QUESTIONS FOR CHAPTER 11

Do you contemplate anyone in your life? Try it with someone dear to you. With whom is it easy? Can you make it habitual?

What happens when you contemplate strangers, people at work? Does it change your perception of people?

In the story of the father and daughter in conflict, what changed?

Contemplate someone with whom you experience tension or conflict. What happens?

# Contemplating Ourselves  12

THE GREAT COMMANDMENT tells us to love our neighbor as ourselves. This implies that we must love ourselves with a healthy, self-accepting love if our neighbors are to experience a comparable love from us. Such love must be learned and cultivated with care.

We take our cues from our parents, relatives, teachers and associates. As children, we, typically, were affirmed and encouraged. As we grew into puberty, we often were insecure about our bodies and struggled for independence from our parents. Affirmation often vanished, replaced with parental lectures and warnings.

"Helpful" criticism abounded, but little praise. Adult censures found ready support in the lack of self-worth already felt, even when we covered up our feelings.

In former days, parental authority was reinforced by religious teaching which was far more eloquent of our sinfulness than of our goodness. God was portrayed as a good and loving Creator who, nevertheless, was a stern judge who kept careful track of our sins.

The result of this self-deprecation was that many people of faith entered adult life with low self-esteem.

This was especially true of young women. They were taught to be self-effacing. Unlike young men, they received little encouragement for achievement. Women were trained to be good mothers and docile wives, obedient to their husbands and to the Church.

Religious educators, reflecting the Second Vatican Council, have profoundly changed the way in which children are taught about God. God is portrayed as a deeply caring parent who created them in love and wants them to grow and to be blessed. We are summoned by God to use our gifts to love one another and to help create a more just and shared world.

In spite of these changes, young people today still struggle for self-esteem and face a pervasive anxiety that violence in the streets or schools may end their lives prematurely. Teenage suicides, second only to accidents as a cause of young deaths, are but one mirror of the struggles of growing up with healthy self-love today.

Contemplating ourselves is an integral part of noisy contemplation. It is an effort to view ourselves with an honest, loving gaze that reflects the perspective of God.

Such a view rejects self-deprecation as contrary to our faith. We are "heirs of heaven," as St. Paul said, beloved sons and daughters of God (Gal. 4). Jesus died to set us free.

*Building the Habit*

Contemplation of ourselves often feels strange when we first attempt it. Although we think about ourselves, worry about our appearance, what we wear and what we say, we seldom just look at ourselves with an open heart to see the person whom God loves. Perhaps we are afraid we'll be overwhelmed by our deficiencies.

We need to work self-contemplation into our praying. A morning greeting at the mirror can initiate this prayer as we begin the day.

This contemplative gaze can return to ourselves at brief moments during the course of the day with an encouragement to open our hearts to people around us, as did Jesus. These moments of self-contemplation, repeated frequently, can shape a habit of contemplating ourselves in the midst of busy lives.

Experience suggests that longer sessions of self-contemplation often alternate between contemplation and self-analysis. Contemplation, with its open gaze, is not judgmental, although it often communicates profound insights and judgments. Self-analysis tends to settle on a particular facet of our life and seeks the "whys" and "wherefores" of our actions.

The two dynamics can be mutually supportive, helping us to interpret our lives and using contemplation's larger perspective to locate ourselves against a backdrop of faith. We are loved by God, liberated by Christ, guided by the Spirit and called to spread the Good News in our world.

Backed by such a divine "vote of confidence," we may feel empowered to deal with daily living.

In the early stories, Sarah, with her feelings of doubt and self-rejection, may find such prayer reassuring. It has power to confront self-deprecation and to challenge any feelings of smugness. Self-contemplation holds us in the perspective of God's love.

The following exercise may help to illustrate this point:

*Choose a favored Scripture passage in which Jesus is ministering to people. The Sermon on the Mount (Mt. 5–7), the feeding of the five thousand (Lk. 9), or some other passage will serve.*

*Read the Gospel passage and use your imagination to be present to what is happening.*

*Put yourself among the crowd or be one of Jesus' disciples. Use your various senses to see, hear and feel what is taking place. Spend some time watching Jesus.*

*Now reverse the tables and take on the eyes of Jesus.*

*Look out on the crowd to where you are sitting or standing. Try to feel how Jesus would perceive you.*

*Whom would he see? How would he react when he saw you?*

*Come up close and greet Jesus, maybe even exchange a hug of greeting. Can you manage that?*

**CONCLUSION:** To love ourselves is a vital requirement if we are to love our neighbors as ourselves.

Contemplation of ourselves is the opposite of religious narcissism or "navel gazing." Far from yielding self-glorification or adulation, contemplation of ourselves reaps a typical harvest of encouragement and honesty in accepting our faults and in using our talents. We grow deeply conscious of God's love for us. The experience frees us to return that love to God and to other people.

# STUDY QUESTIONS FOR CHAPTER 12

What happens when you contemplate yourself? Can you do it easily?

Do the exercise with Jesus. How far from Jesus did you find yourself? What does this say about the way you relate to Jesus?

# Contemplating God  13

C ENTRAL TO OUR life of faith is our quest to establish contact with the living God. The search for God is full of paradoxes. To honor God, countless people have waged war and slaughtered brothers and sisters.

Yet, for many people, the search for God has brought great joy and holiness, led them to love other people and encouraged them to forgive injuries. Faith in God has always had implications for human lives. Faith in a personal God can make radical claims on the way we live. The expressions of this faith have been as varied as the people who believed.

Maximillian Kolbe took the place of a married man in the Nazi gas chamber. Thomas Merton sought out the cloister. Countless parents have been more loving of their children. Multitudes have attended church and studied the Scriptures. Some have given up dancing, while David danced more joyfully. Martyrs have fallen and believers have risen. All have been touched by their faith in God.

Millennia of searching and reflection still leave us with the essential mystery of God. Responses to our belief in God are acts of faith, no matter how much religious institutions may claim to know the mind of God.

Thus, prayer, the dialogue of faith, is a vital endeavor for a person who believes or who seeks to believe.

Yet how do we approach a mysterious, unseen God?

*Salvation History*

An oversimplified, somewhat whimsical version of salvation history might go like this.

For millions of years, as the human race evolved, God watched contentedly as the beloved creatures explored their earth, discovered their gifts and pondered the mysteries of their existence. Various forces of life were worshipped and placated. Human beings acknowledged many spirits or gods.

Finally, in the midst of the mystery which is our universe, God made a self-revelation to a small and insignificant tribe in the Near East.

Our God is personal, all-powerful, all-knowing and just. But this God is also deeply loving, merciful and respectful of all creation and the complex dynamics by which it moves and develops.

God especially reverenced the freedom with which each person was created, although in the Old Testament, God had an enormous struggle to rein in divine power and a longing to control human beings. Countless parents have faced the same challenge with their children.

Thus, throughout the Old Testament, God came to Israel as the mighty God who created the universe, the powerful God who called them out of Egypt in the face of Pharaoh's resistance.

God was the fierce God who demanded that they worship no other gods. God slew or exiled them when they were unfaithful to the covenant which God made with them.

Their God was a patriarchal God, able to protect them from hostile tribes and evil spirits.

Yet flashes of a gentler side to God peeked through. Although angry with human beings and their evil, God saved Noah with the people and the animals of the Ark, so that human beings could try again to get it right.

Abraham could coax God not to destroy an evil city if even a few just people could be found.

God loved tenderly, mercifully and faithfully, even after the beloved people repeatedly were unfaithful. God brought them back from exile in Babylon to their own cherished land and promised them a Messiah.

Yet God found that close, personal relationships with human beings were hard to achieve. No matter how hard God tried to relate to them, people found it difficult to respond to a being so different from themselves.

God was so powerful, while they felt powerless; so know-it-all, when they were so dumb; so invulnerable, when they were so fragile; so self-sufficient, while they needed help for everything.

It was an unequal match. Like young people, constantly lectured on how much gratitude they owed their parents, the Israelites often rebelled against a relationship in which they could never be equals. It might be great to have an all-powerful bodyguard when times were rough, but what a bore when things were going well, to have to bow and scrape so that God would feel respected. So God decided to try a different approach.

Perhaps God wanted some first-hand experience of what it's like to be a human being, to have limits and to have to struggle with good and evil. Perhaps God, observing that human beings love most deeply when they share more equality, wanted to be loved selflessly, not just for the benefits that people expected. Perhaps God wanted to experiment with better ways of saving people so that the methods could be used on other planets. Perhaps Jesus just wanted to travel.

*The Way Recommended by God*

In the most profound lifestyle change that any person has ever experienced, God became a human being, Jesus. From immortal, to mortal; from all knowing, to a learner; from all powerful, to human and limited; from needing no one, to needing human love and nurturing; from independent of all creation, to dependent on parents, friends and the bounty of the earth – God was finally walking in our sandals.

Jesus became one of us by passing through the journey each of us must make. He was conceived, born and raised as a human being, knowing the joys and sadness, the labor and the pride of toil, the joy of love and friendship, the agony of a friendship betrayed.

Not until late middle age, by the limited life span of those days, did he begin a public ministry among the ordinary people and the outcasts of his land. A few disciples followed him and crowds gathered.

Certain wonders took place: stories of healing, casting out demons, blind people seeing, deaf people hearing, lame people walking and a few dead people returning to life.

But the wonders were shyly offered, not flaunted or used to force people to believe. He taught in murky stories. The ministry was so focused among the lower classes of Israel that most opinion makers and "power people" spurned him. Eventually they decided that he was disturbing their peace and had him killed.

He wouldn't stay dead. His disciples claimed that he rose and reappeared to them, telling them to carry on his work. They spread his teaching, first to Jewish communities and then to Gentiles. Vast expansion took place.

Communities gathered about the bread and wine they called the Eucharist, told stories of Jesus' life and welcomed people with a love that was warm and willing to pay prices. Many died for their faith. Certain writers described what they knew of Jesus. The testimonials that survived became the New Testament, which, together with the Old Testament, form the Scriptures of our faith. Although the books about Jesus are brief, centuries of people have found them a gentle invitation to dance the mystery. We are invited, but never coerced, into following Jesus.

Thus Jesus became the way of faith recommended by God. Revelation had put on a human face. A person who was both God and one of us became the bridge across the chasm between God and human beings.

By contemplating and loving Jesus, we share this mysterious crossing and build personal relationships with God.


*Contemplating Jesus in the Scriptures*

Reading a Gospel story of Jesus and entering into the scene is an ancient and powerful dynamic of contemplation. In our imagination, we can be present, hear again the words, see the place and watch Jesus preach and interact with people. Feeling his impact upon the people, we can open our hearts to this person who was both God and one of us in all ways.

Contemplative prayer based upon reading and pondering the Scriptures can help us, as the prayer echoed in *Godspell* says, to "see thee more clearly, love thee more dearly, follow thee more nearly, day by day." Praying over Jesus in the Scriptures is a primary way for us to build habits of noisy contemplation.

Through contemplating the Scriptures, we come to know what Jesus was like as a human being, how he related to people, how he handled life.

We meet the activist, busy about God's work. We experience the contemplative love with which he met people and which nourished and sustained him. We experience the texture of his preaching, ministry and life of the person whom we follow.

The Scriptures are basic to our life of faith and prayer.

### Meeting Jesus in the Eucharist

The Eucharist is another major font of Christian prayer. For countless people, celebrating the Eucharist has revealed Christ to them just as surely as the breaking of the bread revealed him to the depressed disciples who had walked unseeing with him on the road to Emmaus (Lk. 24:31).

The Eucharist has been an experience of contemplative learning for people who could not understand the language. With eyes of faith, centuries of believers drew nourishment and piety from the upraised host and cup at the consecration and felt solidarity of hearts with the community that worshipped.

The Eucharist, like all good liturgy, is essentially a contemplative event, a service whose signs and symbols communicate beyond the scope of the words.

Thus we pray it most deeply when we take part contemplatively, participating with attention and energy. The secrets of the Eucharist are not unlocked to people who approach it in the detached fashion of observers, or who worship as a prayer of individual piety.

The Eucharist is a contemplative mystery revealed to those who participate, people who sing, pray, listen and invest themselves in the sharing.

**OBSERVATION:** Given the contemplative power of the Eucharist and its rightful place at the center of the Christian community, it is unfortunate that as we priests age and decline in numbers, communities are being left without the Eucharist rather than allowed Eucharistic ministry from married people and from women.

Perhaps it is no surprise that a merry God is calling forth the most powerful growth of Christian communities in lands where priests are least plentiful or in rapid decline. Perhaps, like John the Baptist, we priests must decrease so that the ministry of Christ through the people may increase.

## Meeting Christ in Other People

Christians have been encouraged to see Christ in other people. Although, as noted before, Christ seems not to have prayed this way, the practice contains a powerful core of insight.

When we meet another person in a loving way, the experience can communicate Christ's love and presence. If we welcome people and contemplate them, the encounters will show us God's creative hand and Christ's saving love at work, i.e., we will meet Christ in others.

The practice would become a barrier if we came to human encounters with an awareness of Christ held before us to shield us from experiencing and bonding with the people we meet. We would be using Christ to buffer ourselves from the realities and love of our world.

The nuance is careful, but important. Love for God is not a retreat from, but an empowerment for loving our neighbors, especially the poor. If we open our hearts to our neighbors, our awareness of Christ will flourish.

### Contemplating God Directly

As we encounter Jesus, we often experience the truth of Jesus' words that if we know him, we know God and have seen God, for he is in God and God is in him (Jn. 14:7-10).

As part of our prayer, we can cultivate a direct experience of God. This generally occurs, not with images of God, but with an abiding, loving presence whom we associate with God.

This presence of God is a contemplative experience, grasped with our inner senses through our faith. Only faith can interpret this presence as an encounter with God.

But our awareness of God's presence can be nurtured to grow more habitual, just as people who love one another can nourish the habit of being present to the person they love. We need to spend time with God.

We do that by reminding ourselves of God's love for us and of the way God holds us in love. God can be a word that we carry through the day in our hearts, like the simplest form of the "Jesus" prayer, when we carry that word and repeat it throughout the day.

As we spend time with God, God becomes an illuminating presence in our lives, warming dark recesses of our hearts and encouraging us to love more deeply.

Our awareness of God's presence in our lives can exist in the midst of busy activity, not shutting out, but enlarging our contemplation of other people and of the earth around us.

## What Should Happen?

Although the problem is not unique to us, the very simplicity of enjoying God's presence poses a challenge for North Americans. We are used to "doing things," making things happen, being active, keeping busy.

Simply dwelling in God's presence and resting contented in God's love are such simple experiences that we wonder about their value. We want to know, "What's happening? What should we expect? Is it worthwhile?"

The test is the slow impact such prayer has upon our lives. Contemplating God and contemplating people are experiences of love. When the love we share is the realistic, strong and durable love described earlier, then abiding in such love will slowly work its alchemy upon our lives and love for others.

## Seeking Peace & Serenity

A further question should be raised. Are peace and serenity the necessary preparation for prayer, or are peace and serenity the result of our prayer? Phrased differently: Do we seek stillness and quiet in order to pray, or do we pray in order to find peace?

Earlier ages, as previously noted, assumed that deep prayer required a physical environment that was peaceful, and a psychic condition that was detached and serene. Prayerful people sought tranquility. These conditions were deemed essential. Thus people who lacked the environment were excluded from deep prayer.

This assumed exclusion from deep prayer because of lack of proper environment is illustrated by a young woman who, when she first heard of noisy contemplation, exploded in frustration, "I went 16 years to Catholic schools, from grade school through college, and not one person ever talked to me about growing deeply prayerful!"

Contemplative bonding with God, although able to be nourished in special ways when we step aside from busy lives, can also flourish in the midst of the busyness. God is not constrained in loving us.

As salvation history has pointed out, God can be as noisy as is necessary to get our attention. Whether it be Yahweh's shaking of Mt. Horeb, the parting of the Red Sea, the use of angelic messengers and dreams or in speaking "Jesus," the Word of God, to our world, God can communicate with us in a spectrum of voices that range from silence to thunder.

Jesus sought silent nights and hills as a place for prayer and perspective. Jesus prayed his fears in the Garden in order to find serenity and courage for his noisy, anxious heart. But throughout most of his ministry, loving and praying took place as he shared life with the people.

Thus, just as stillness offers a path to God, so too can we experience God in the midst of our noisy lives. No matter what be our environment and psychic state, prayer is open to every person.

# STUDY QUESTIONS FOR CHAPTER 13

How do you find God most easily? What does this
tell you about the way that you pray? Build upon your
strengths.

Do you read the Scriptures very often? Try reading a
story of Jesus ministering, and try to become present to
the scene.

Would reading a story a day be a good way to build a
habit of contemplating Jesus?

# Contemplating Society: 14
## Loving Distant Neighbors

**W**E'VE TALKED OF contemplating God, contemplating ourselves, contemplating nature and of contemplating people with whom we share life – our near neighbors.

Let us now consider our contemplation of distant neighbors, sisters and brothers known to us only as classes of people, races, genders, communities or members of other nations. In such prayer, we reach out to people who have no names or faces for us but whom our faith tells us are loved by God and redeemed by Jesus Christ. Jesus' life and ministry, reflected in the call of the church, urges us to show a special love for poor people.

The poor are brothers and sisters who have a claim to the earth that is equal to our own. But, whereas more advantaged people can use their resources to exert some control over their destiny, poor people have no power and few options.

Early Christians remembered Christ's example that community and solidarity of hearts was the greatest gift they had to offer those who were poorer than they were. Their charity and hospitality drew people to the community.

To build this community of Jesus' followers in our own day, we must both cherish local communities and work in solidarity to overcome the sinful social structures of this earth, the injustices that they support and the personal selfishness which they spawn.

### Linking Life to the Scriptures

A community of women religious on retreat was praying over the passage where Jesus is asleep in the boat while his disciples grow fearful that they will perish in the storm (Mk. 4:35-41).

They put themselves in the boat with the disciples, experienced the wind and the waves, the terror of impending death and the grateful but shocked relief when Jesus stilled the waves.

Since it was 1978, the time when the "boat people" were beginning to stream out of Vietnam, these women religious then imagined themselves in one of the leaky, overcrowded boats facing the weather and pirates of the South China Sea.

They joined people crying out to "Christian" nations, especially to the United States, asking us to wake up and help them before they perished.

The double-sided contemplation was a deep experience. They followed up by contacting their local representative urging favorable u.s. welcome for the "boat people." They became a source of support and encouragement for refugee resettlement in their local towns.

These women were contemplating society.

In more recent days you might contemplate the people of Haiti fleeing in boats to escape the wrenching poverty only to be seized and sent back by the u.s. Coast Guard.

## The Heritage

The experience of the church community in the days since Jesus died have conditioned the way Christians approach society.

Whereas early Christians were expansionist, welcoming people to the community and seeking to embrace the people of the world, later centuries grew protectionist, seeking to prevent corruption by the "world," now viewed as dangerous. Religion and worldly affairs were best left unmixed. The "City of God" and "City of Man" were to be kept apart.

By the Middle Ages, the church was expansionist again and garnered sizable control over European society.

The Reformation wars cut back this control, even though missionaries spread through the newly discovered world. Church and state in many lands reached an accommodation that left each with a sphere of influence into which the other might venture only at its peril.

"Separation of church and state," the political option in the United States, encouraged u.s. citizens to believe that faith was a private affair. The church should deal with moral questions, comfort people and nourish piety. Civil society should not interfere in church life.

The late 20th century saw a rebirth of awareness that our faith is both personal and public. Numerous Popes and religious leaders have stressed that faith and love have implications for society.

Tension over the proper relationship of religious faith and social structures continues.

Fundamentalists seek to impose Islamic rule on Moslem lands. The Vatican tries to implement its moral agenda and expand its sway in national political life. Church leaders such as Romero are assassinated or threatened with death because they walk with poor people and defend their right to redress centuries of injustice. The u.s. Congress and courts are urged to restore prayer in the public schools and to outlaw abortion. Church leaders lobby for government funds for 'faith based' initiatives.

Religious beliefs and the way they are acted out have a profound impact upon human society.

## The Call to Societal Love

Societal consciousness and a concern for justice have only recently moved from the periphery to the center of Roman Catholic spirituality. It has lagged behind the "social Gospel" preaching of Protestant churches.

Church social teaching, revived by Leo xiii and developed by Pius xi and Pius xii, received powerful impetus from John xxiii and the Second Vatican Council. Paul vi, John Paul ii and bishops throughout the world, especially those of Latin America at Medellin and Puebla, have stressed that God seeks to liberate people from personal sin and from social injustice.

Document after document (often so challenging that North American clergy have not preached them) has proclaimed the church's solidarity with the people of God, "especially those who are poor or in any way oppressed" (*Church in the Modern World*, no. 1). By our faith, we are called to work for justice, to love society and the people of the earth.

*The Societal Challenge to Prayer & Spirituality*

The problem with this renewed call to Christian involvement in society is that little spiritual reflection has been devoted to prayer which supports such activity.

The experience of many prayerful people testifies that models of prayer, based on silence and separation, are inadequate to deal with the stresses introduced by our struggles to alleviate human misery and injustice.

Trusting that the Church's societal "call to action" is not a summons to religious destruction, but a path to religious empowerment and a closer following of Jesus, we must build habits of prayer which will sustain our societal love and commitment. A major support in prayer for a life of justice is to contemplate distant neighbors.

## Contemplating Distant Neighbors

When we contemplate Jesus in the Scriptures, we use our imagination to enter into the Gospel story. Events that happened in the past now live for us in our prayer.

When a person whom we love is distant, our contemplative imagination can make them present and deepen our love.

Contemplation of God can bring a feeling of God's presence. Even when God seems distant, our prayer is transforming our lives in the way that time spent sharing love nourishes human hearts. As the fox tells the Little Prince of the value of his rose:

*"I will make you a present of a secret," said the fox. "It is only with the heart that one can see rightly; what is essential is invisible to the eye... It is the time you have wasted for your rose that makes your rose so important."*
— *The Little Prince*, Antoine de Saint Exupéry, p. 86.

So it is that we can use our contemplative imagination to experience and bond with sisters and brothers in other areas and lands. We can spend time with them and join them in solidarity of hearts. Our sharing may find ways to express our love.

Even when no overt actions are possible, the solidarity we share in prayer can make a difference. It is the difference experienced by a person who suffers alone in a hospital bed, compared to a person who suffers equal pain but has someone nearby who loves them.

So for us, the power of our prayer can send our love to others and transform our own hearts on the journey.

*Where Do We Begin?*

Societal prayer begins just as does prayer over the Scriptures. We must know something about the situation we wish to contemplate. The knowledge need not be extensive, only sufficient to enter into their experience.

Let's take some examples:

### 1 BOSNIA AND HERZEGOVINA

In Bosnia the Serbs, Croats and Muslims have been locked in a complex political-ethnic-religious struggle. The conflict resurrected historical rivalries and wellsprings of hostility that political leaders use to carry out savage attacks, the so-called "ethnic cleansing" of opponents.

While timid international efforts at peace flickered and repeatedly died, the violence went on, a grim reaper whose daily diet of wounded, raped, brutalized and dying reached enormous totals.

To contemplate this experience we can join in our imagination with the inhabitants of Sarajevo, or Goražde. Experience the chronic fear that stalked the streets and homes, rising each time the boom of a heavy artillery shell arose from the surrounding hills, relaxing in macabre relief only when the whistle of the shell and exploding debris signaled that the shell fell in some other neighborhood. Once again, we and our children had survived.

You might explore this besieged suffering against a background of Jesus' preaching of the beatitudes (Mt. 5:1-12).

## 2 SOUTH AFRICA

Our imagination and empathy can take us to South Africa where recent elections ended decades of harsh discrimination from white people who exploited the labor of black people and crushed their dreams of freedom with the harsh and arbitrary police power of the apartheid system.

We can feel the anger of newly triumphant blacks whose vast vote for Nelson Mandela and the African National Congress stirs the temptation to wreak vengeance on the white minority who quoted Scripture to justify the separation of the races, the dominance of the white community and its exploitation of black people.

Enter into the feelings of recently empowered black parents who live with apartheid's memory of watching their children go hungry, lack education and die, while white families lived affluent lives and sent their healthy children to splendid schools.

In your contemplative imagination, become an Afrikaner of conscience who prays over Christ's great commandment (Mt. 22:37-38). What are your attitudes toward people whose skin color differs from your own? Do you help to justify Gandhi's poignant words, "I love your Christ, but I hate your Christians."

We can also be present to Afrikaners who dreaded the moment of black empowerment and saw it as the loss of everything they held precious. How like the Christian community in Acts 15. Many Jewish followers of Jesus were sure that all was ruined when the community decided to let the Gentile converts join without requiring them to become Jews. Time would prove them wrong, but at the moment their hearts must have been heavy, indeed.

### 3 NICARAGUA: MOTHERS OF MATAGALPA

Societal contemplations are not all sadness and suffering. As Christ predicted, faith can transform suffering.

In the mountain town of Matagalpa, a group of Sandinista Mothers whose children had been killed by contras were praying over Jesus words, "Love your enemies. Do good to those who hate you" (Lk. 6:27). Their discussion quickly named as their enemies the contra fighters and families responsible for the death of their children. They decided that Jesus was calling them to forgive and seek reconciliation with their enemies.

The Mothers arranged a meeting with some contra mothers, discovered common needs for housing, food and jobs and a willingness to try to be reconciled for the sake of their children.

They decided to attempt to build a 150-home "City of Hope and Reconciliation," where half of the community would be Sandinista mothers and disabled Sandinista soldiers and half would be contra mothers and disabled former contra fighters. They began to build the community.

The Mothers project stirred similar, smaller efforts in Nicaragua. The original project fell apart in a political conflict that paralyzed and fragmented the community. Heroic ventures that are attempted by humans often fall apart, yet the dream was a mighty one and is still remembered.

Use your contemplative imagination to enter into the feelings of parents whose children have been killed by opposing forces.

* What does it take to forgive political opponents who killed your children?
* Who are your enemies?
* Can you respond to Jesus' challenge to love your enemies?
* What holds you back?

### 4 AN URBAN PARENT WITH TEENAGE CHILDREN

Use your imagination to bond with Mary, a working mother with two teenage children, the result of an early marriage to a man who beat her regularly and abused the children until she got up the courage to defy his threats and leave.

Mary worked her way off welfare through education and low-paying jobs until she became an executive secretary in a nearby business. The family is just making it.

Kathy and Tom, her children, are teenagers, sophomore and junior respectively, attending a public high school, where four students have been expelled this year for bringing in guns. One student has been killed and one committed suicide.

Mary has tried to be a good mother, but the strain of juggling too many responsibilities takes its toll. Tom sometimes hangs out with a tough crowd and wonders if he'll have a future. Kathy is vivacious and Mary is constantly encouraging her to resist the pressures to experiment with sex.

The death of a young neighbor with AIDS last year was a somber reminder. Mary prays that her children will be spared the street violence and sexual disease that are so common in the neighborhood. Maybe someday they'll be able to move out.

Bond with the struggle that present-day parents face throughout the world.

## 5 PEOPLE IN HOSPITALS

Most of us dread hospitals and avoid them until we are forced to.

Yet, we can visit in our imagination with people who suffer, especially those who have no one to care about them.

Contemplate also the people who care for them: doctors, nurses and service workers who staff the institution.

We can link our prayer with passages which describe Jesus' ministry of healing such as in Lk. 5:12-16 or 5:17-26.

The compassion that flows from such prayer can deepen our awareness of suffering and send the energy of our love to aid people who are ill. This prayer can bring patience for and sensitivity to problems of ill health in our own families. It can prepare us for illness in our own lives.

Today, when ministry to the sick is one of the most rapidly expanding ministries in our church, this prayer might encourage us to explore our own involvement.

## 6 UNEMPLOYMENT

Joe Smith spent 30 years on the auto assembly line. Celeste, his wife is a secretary. Together they earned in excess of $70,000, with full benefits.

They've worked hard and tried to bring up the three kids to be decent, honest people. They paid their taxes and complained about the lazy people who would rather be on welfare or unemployment than work.

And now it has hit them. The factory has closed, laying off 7,000. Foreign autos now dominate the market. Celeste and Joe are trying to make it on her salary and his unemployment checks. Middle class dreams have vanished in the struggle to make ends meet. The mortgage on the house has 10 years to run. The credit card debt is mounting.

Joe has put on fruitless miles looking for work in the area, but so have most of the other 7,000 who were laid off, plus those lopped off by the subcontractors who served the big plant.

How could it happen to them? Why are they fighting so much and squabbling in the family just when they need to pull together?

Try contemplating Celeste and Joe's plight, typical of so many people. Enter into the anxieties they feel.

You might contemplate sisters and brothers of poor nations who often face 25–50 percent unemployment, not just for short periods of time, but for most of their lives. They worry, just as we do, and grieve when people they love suffer and die from lack of food or health care. They try to live, love their children and seek happiness, just as we do.

Psalm 31 and Luke 12:22-32 on God's love for us might offer a context for such praying.

## 7  PRAYING THE FUTURE

Just as contemplation can reach into the past, so also it can envision the future. It is not necessarily prophetic but, indeed, may prepare our hearts.

Try contemplating a church where people treat one another as equals, where discrimination has been eliminated and where each person serves the community according to her or his gifts. Perhaps you might contemplate a worship service in such a community. What is it like?

St. Paul can provide a Scriptural reflection: "All (are) baptized in Christ, you have all clothed yourselves in Christ and there are no more distinctions between Jew and Greek, slave and free, male and female, but all of you are one in Christ Jesus" (Gal. 3:27-28).

*Societal Awareness: Can We Bear It?*

The initial response to societal contemplation, reinforced by the examples given, can be: "Who needs it?" "I've got troubles enough of my own." "I feel powerless enough without asking for more grief."

Only experience can convince us of the power which such prayer possesses to nourish, integrate and enrich our lives. Our prayer over the Gospel gives us some experience of this.

When we contemplate Christ in the Scriptures, especially in his passion, we find that the love and compassion which such prayer stirs in our hearts encourages us to risk Christ's words, "My yoke is easy and my burden light" (Mt. 11:30).

Societal contemplation expands our hearts just as surely as does contemplation of people and prayer over the Scriptures. All are part of life in the great commandment.

Sharing the concerns of distant sisters and brothers brings perspective to our own lives. Solidarity of hearts encourages us to work for an earth that is peaceful, shared, just and loving.

## Contemplating the News

Most adults in North America however briefly, read a daily paper, check on-line news sources, listen to the radio or watch news on TV. A simple way to build a habit of societal contemplation is to contemplate the news.

It takes no longer to contemplate the news than to read it or watch it. We can use the brief information and images to enter into an experience which someone is facing.

We can grieve with families of accident victims, celebrate with people who escape disaster, and acknowledge the humanness in those we support or oppose in politics. We can reach around the earth to bond with sisters and brothers.

The ongoing struggles and violence smoldering between the Arabs and the Israelis, the suicide bombings, the ever-vigorous sale of weapons, with the U.S. leading the way, the nuclear weapons still poised, those planning to concoct another "9/11" against the U.S., the torture we visit on those we suspect to be "terrorists," the abandonment of our cherished liberties to coerce information out of them – these are struggles that challenge our abilities to call forth reconciliation and to silence the weapons.

Our worldwide need to conserve resources, rein in pollution and halt global warming, the maldistribution of wealth that results in affluence for a few and misery for billions must be faced by people who love enough to confront it boldly with the Gospel's call to peace and who demand other alternatives to resolve human conflicts.

Just as Jacob wrestled through the night with God (Gen. 32), so must we continue to wrestle with the powerful forces that foster the conflicts and reap vast profits from the labor of the poor. Social justice comes from the patient, persevering efforts of people who can keep their gaze fixed on Christ's vision of love and step lightly to the call to bring forth such a world.


### Contemplating the Church: The People of God

We can use our societal gaze to contemplate our church and the strange and wonderful assortment of people who comprise it. St. Paul's vision of the people of God as the Mystical Body of Christ (1 Cor. 12:12-31) is just such a contemplative vista.

Our hearts need not shy away from challenging the sin and selfishness in institutional church life: the secretiveness of our bishops when sexual issues – such as the pedophilia scandal – and embezzlement are exposed, the resistance to sharing power and ministry, the political choices made when Gospel responses are needed, the discrimination toward women, our prejudices toward people of other cultures and faiths.

Contemplation can face the bad as well as the good, for it is a prayer of love. When we treated the church as divine, we were constantly scandalized at our clay-fullness. We now celebrate that the church is fashioned of human beings, who, though limited and capable of sin, offer a community in which Christ's dreams of love often burst into life.

Contemplation can play a powerful ecumenical role. Individuals or whole communities can visit, personally or in imagination, with sisters and brothers who celebrate our faith yet worship Jesus in richly diverse ways. We can behold people who share most of our faith, but belong to other churches. Contemplating and loving the members of other churches is a crucial step toward bridging the gulfs that separate Christians from one another.

Contemplation can let us begin the controversial and highly emotional process of being reconciled with our sisters and brothers in China, the former Soviet Union and Cuba. Whatever the ideological and military security questions that divide our nations, we who follow Christ must love the people. They seek the same security and freedom that we do. Christ called us to peace and love, not war and domination. Contemplation of their lives can diminish our cultural hostilities and open our hearts to the people of these lands.

People who develop this habit may find that their love for the United States grows deeper and more mature. In place of the adolescent posture, "My country right or wrong," can grow an adult gaze which acknowledges our blessings, challenges our failings and calls our leaders to seek not just empowerment and security for ourselves, but freedom, peace and justice for all.

By contemplating at least one or two such situations each day, we can build a habit of societal prayer which will bond us with our sisters and brothers across the world in the way that Christ loved the people of Israel. From communities filled with such love will flow forth Christ's creative ministry for our present day.

# STUDY QUESTIONS FOR CHAPTER 14

Have you ever had an experience of loving "distant neighbors?" What was it like?

Use your imagination to visit some of the examples described. What happens when you contemplate them?

Try to contemplate some item from the TV news or newspaper each day. What happens?

Try contemplating the church. What do you see?

# Contemplation 15
## and Conflict

Human love, lived out in a limited and sinful world, stirs conflicts and raises tensions while it also nourishes our hearts. Not all tensions are unwelcome. Some are socially acceptable and focus energy creatively that might otherwise be expressed destructively.

Sports lovers relish the Superbowl and the World Series, just as ancient Romans loved gladiators in the Coliseum and races in the Circus Maximus. Many love the challenge of a business deal, passing an exam, trying a new experiment, skiing down a slope, visiting a new place, all the things that people do to vary the ordinariness of existence. Joggers and aerobic dancers enjoy the stretching muscles that signal good health.

But other conflicts and suffering pose deep religious challenges. We fear both conflict itself and the threat of conflict. Unless we have a way to deal with the tensions, we must try to avoid situations that stir them up. Yet, struggle and tension are pervasive in our lives. They extend throughout our efforts to live the great commandment.

We experience tensions with:

*God*

We may love God, yet the mystery of God remains profoundly challenging.

If God is all powerful and all loving, why do babies die? Why do good people suffer while the wicked prosper? Why do our attempts to be loving stir our deepest pain? If Jesus went about doing good, why was he killed?

*Ourselves*

We struggle with self-worth, confidence and trust. We find emotions hard to express. We hurt people we love. We live with unresolved familial conflicts and bitter memories. We're worried about our future, our finances, our survival and our destiny. We struggle with the gap between our dreams of living the Gospel and the way we act. "I fail to carry out the things I want to do, and I find myself doing the very things I hate" (Rom. 7:35).

*People We Love*

We are most vulnerable to those whom we love dearly: family, spouse, children, parents and friends. Conflicts here often sum up relationships, whether it be a spouse exploding over a cap left off a toothpaste tube, or an otherwise mature adult reduced to childhood by a parent who still knows which "button" to push.

*Our Church*

Our religious upbringing leads to tension when we discover that religious leaders who claim to speak for God are as prone to sin as we are, and as prone to love.

We face the credibility gap in our churches. We preach reconciliation, yet show a history of unforgiving conflicts with each other. We preach justice, freedom and human rights to civil governments while often blind to such values in the internal life of our own communities. We support unions everywhere except in church institutions.

*Our Nation*

When we try to live the Gospel, work for justice and reflect Christ's special love for the poor, we threaten existing patterns of society and our efforts are resisted.

To urge our nation to share power and wealth with poorer lands, as Pope Paul VI urged in *Populorum Progressio*, (1967) is to face ridicule. During the 1980s, to work for an end to the contra war in Nicaragua and to the death squads in El Salvador was to be charged with being "dupes of the international communist conspiracy."

Yet, conflict itself is not the only dimension of struggle that we fear. We fear the *threat* of violence and conflict.

*Fears of Conflict*

We fear conflict. A verbal battle leaves us vibrating for hours, even days. A summons from the IRS makes us quake, even though we've never fudged a tax form. A harsh word from the boss gnaws at us for weeks. A fight with the kids leaves parents and children feeling unloved. Anxieties about life lead us to reach for the Valium.

Even the *threat of conflict* can control our behavior. We avoid behavior that might trigger such a struggle.

Threats of conflict deflect us from addressing sensitive questions. "I don't want to talk about it! There will be a fight." People think twice before braving such threats.

We're intimidated by threats to our reputation, prestige, financial or physical security.

The threat of physical violence makes everyone anxious. Women live under the threat of rape. Crime in the streets makes us wary at night. Muggings by young people pressure the elderly. Burglaries lead home owners to mount elaborate security precautions. Terrorism threatens the security of presidents. Neither Pope nor President is immune.

Yet, Jesus encouraged us to risk greatly for the sake of love and not to fear the conflicts that might result. He promised us the Spirit to guide us through the struggles, even the deaths that might result. Jesus walked the path before us and showed us the way.

### Conflict & Contemplation in Jesus' Life

As noted before, Jesus' public ministry was surrounded by tensions and conflict. He disturbed the established order and confronted authorities. Conflict and the threat of conflict were the companions he expected: "Do not suppose that I have come to bring peace to the earth: it is not peace I have come to bring, but a sword" (Mt. 10:34).

Indeed, Jesus' ministry, far from entailing days of pious, playful hiking around Israel, of the type popularized in *Godspell,* was rather a ministry of passionate love and powerful preaching around

NOISY CONTEMPLATION

which swirled threats from people who would ultimately achieve his death.

Jesus suffered deeply because he loved passionately. He experienced the intense emotions, the love, anger, frustration and the sadness common to people willing to pay a price for what they believe and for the people they love.

Jesus directly contemplated his fears and tensions in order to deal with them. He used prayer to gain courage, to integrate his feelings and to give perspective to his decisions in times of conflict. He confronted his death in prayer and found the courage, peace and serenity to go forward.

Jesus prayed his way through his conflicts, and so can we.

## Contemplating Our Struggles

There is something about fear and conflict that encourage us to pray. If we are going to pray for God's help, we will do it then. "No atheists in the foxholes" contains a strong measure of truth.

A powerful means to personal integration is to contemplate our struggles. Instead of trying to avoid, ignore, bargain away or grow angry with our struggles, we can turn and face them directly, just as people threatened with death move through comparable stages of grieving before accepting what lies ahead.

When we contemplate our conflicts or the threat of conflict, dramatic changes can take place. People often experience marks of God's grace at work: empowerment, perspective, integration and serenity.

### EMPOWERMENT

The very act of facing our struggles is an act of empowerment and self-affirmation. In itself, it often reduces the struggle to more manageable proportions.

### PERSPECTIVE

Our contemplation of conflict and suffering is often suffused with our memory of God's love for us.

### INTEGRATION AND SERENITY

As we contemplate our fears and struggles from the vantage point of faith, a new wholeness and confidence will often emerge. These lead to new serenity and inner peace. Burdens that seemed crushing suddenly become bearable, even easy.

Thus, feelings of conflict, anger and guilt can be made bearable when we simply sit with the feelings, gaze at them and accept them swirling within us. We can remind ourselves that God watches over us. The feelings and inner turmoil are part of us. We have nothing to fear and much to gain by facing them. Roosevelt was right, "We have nothing to fear but fear itself."

*Further Applications*

We've already talked about contemplating ourselves, contemplating God, contemplating people whom we love, including those with whom we need reconciliation, and contemplating society where the vision involves pain and suffering. We can move further and apply this prayer to our memories, and to unresolvable conflicts.

*Contemplating Memories*

Just as joyful memories can be relived, painful memories can be healed by contemplating them.

Contemplation of our memories can help us gain new perspective on the past. When we contemplate our memories, recalling the events on which we wish to focus, we bring a maturity garnered in intervening years and mingle it with the special insights of our contemplation to produce a new perspective.

**EXAMPLE:** During a seminar, a man tried contemplating his father, a person who had died many years before at a time when the very strict father and rebellious son had been locked in deep and unresolved conflict. Death had come so swiftly that no reconciliation had been possible. The memories festered.

While contemplating his father, the son had a sudden insight that his father's strictness and tightly structured life had been a defense against his insecurities and fears of economic failure.

The man suddenly understood his father. The smoldering anger dissolved. He experienced an awareness of his father's goodness and love for him and for the family. The son was filled with peace and love for the first time in many years.

*Unresolvable Conflicts*

In many conflicts we have no power to effect reconciliation with anyone.

**EXAMPLE:** A worker who is fired usually has little redress but to leave with feelings of hurt and outrage. There may not have been any personal focus for the separation, just a pink slip at the hands of a personnel manager during a business retrenchment.

Yet, people are scarred by the experience. They make themselves the focus of their anger, attacking their sense of self-worth.

At such times, we must effect healing in our own hearts. Noisy contemplation can start this healing process.

We can contemplate ourselves against the backdrop of Christ's testimony that we are more treasured by God than the sparrows of the air or the lilies of the field. We can look at our lives, the people with whom we share life and count the blessings we have.

We can also look directly at the bitterness and hurt and acknowledge how normal it is to grieve. We can offer the pain in solidarity with others who face similar pain.

Contemplation can set us on the road to healing. It can be a powerful part of the reconciliation process which may take not just a few, but many moments of such prayer to drain the hurts and effect full healing.

The process of contemplating the conflict offers a powerful way to avoid closing ourselves to festering bitterness. It encourages us to open our hearts to the life that lies ahead.

CONCLUSION: Just as Jesus used prayer to deal with conflict, so we too can pray the struggles of our lives.

As we grow confident that we can work our way through both our fears of conflict and the struggles themselves, the way is open for us to love more deeply.

We grow more free to follow Jesus, even along the way of the cross. It is a path that leads to God, to deep and passionate love for our family and friends, to deep love for the world in which we live and to deep love for ourselves.

# STUDY QUESTIONS FOR CHAPTER 15

Do you have a conflict situation in your life? What happens when you simply sit and gaze at the situation and the people involved?

Try visiting your memories, both the happy ones and the painful ones. Do they change?

# Spiritual Direction for 16
# People of Few Resources

TRADITIONAL CONTEMPLATIVE PRAYER laid great stress upon the importance of spiritual direction for people who pray regularly.

Spiritual directors were spiritual guides, people wise in the ways of prayer, who "directed" the prayerful person in the proper ways to approach God. The person was expected to be perfectly docile to the spiritual director. Better a wise director than a holy one, said St. Teresa of Avila.

Spiritual direction has been renewed in recent years using the insights of psychology. Professional spiritual directors have been trained in counseling, discernment and spiritual growth.

A spiritual director now is more "non-directive," someone trained in the human sciences and in spirituality with whom one can share the experiences of praying and reflect on their meaning.

However, the training of spiritual directors is costly. There are few available and they spend most of their time serving "professionals" in the church – the members of religious communities. The cost of spiritual direction for millions of people in the church would be prohibitive in the present model.

Yet, to share one's prayer and journey in faith with another is of great value. Faith is more properly a collective journey, not a private one. "Companionship for the journey" would be a blessing. How can this sharing be achieved?

*Keeping a Journal*

The simplest companion or aid to our memory is a diary or journal to record significant moments. If used regularly, it can record and retain our memories of the special ways that God's Spirit comes to us. It can describe our personal salvation history, our own scripture.

A few moments of reflection each day, noting any significant experiences or insights, can fix the memories of our prayer. What were the special moments of joy and love? What repels me? Where do I feel strong attraction or aversion? Where do I need reconciliation? What passages in the Scriptures touch me? Where do I feel a call to reach out to others?

Reviewing the journal will reveal common threads that are emerging and suggest directions for our prayer. Keeping a journal is the simplest of ways to find direction for our prayer. It helps us to remember our prayer, perceive our growth and development and read the signs which emerge.

*Companions for the Journey*

A journal is a good resource and, with the guidance of God's Spirit, a powerful one. But faith needs a community to grow to maturity. How can this be achieved?

The most treasured and dynamic way of remembering and understanding is to find a friend with whom we can share, mutually and regularly, the experiences of our journeys in noisy contemplation.

The very telling of our mutual stories illumines our own minds with what is happening. The disciples on the road to Emmaus finally recognized Jesus in the breaking of the bread after their afternoon of dialogue with Jesus had refreshed their memories about what to expect from the Messiah.

The mutual celebration of stories between companions is the simplest of all communal models for spiritual direction, upon which further sharing can be built. Companions can encourage each other and nurture one another's faith.

We can encourage every person who tries noisy contemplation to ask a friend to share the experience. Traveling the journey, two by two, as Christ sent out the early disciples, they can pray, share and celebrate together.

If these companions within a faith community gathered periodically in larger groups to share their experiences, a community, such as a parish, would have a rich source of testimony of God's Spirit acting in their midst.


*Spiritual Direction*

When people begin to pray more deeply it is a blessing to have trained spiritual guides to support them along the way.

Perhaps we might draw on the ideas by which Mao approached Chinese health care.

Looking at the almost one billion Chinese, he saw their poverty, yet also saw their great need for health care. He articulated a model that said, "Everyone needs health care. No one may have a lot until everyone has some." Thus China began its great experiment with "barefoot doctors." A cadre of almost a million Chinese were trained to administer simple drugs which treated the bulk of common ailments. They fanned out over China to give rudimentary health care.

The vision was that each year the "barefoot doctors" would be further upgraded until at the end of fifty years, the health care system would be well developed and the entire people would reach their goal together. Professional doctors and hospitals would serve as centers to handle cases beyond the resources of the local people.

Might we apply this model to spiritual direction?

## Local Spiritual Directors

These local directors are the key to any effort to spread spiritual direction through our communities.

Local directors would begin with brief instruction in the skills of listening, support and discernment. Their ministry is to serve in their local communities as people who support those who pray.

As the experience of local directors grows, professional directors could provide regular discussion and instruction, enabling the local directors to expand their knowledge and skills. Over the years, the corps of local directors would develop great expertise.

## Professional Spiritual Directors

There is still a great need for professional spiritual directors – not to be the primary deliverers of "spiritual health care," but to serve the local spiritual directors and the people who are praying.

Professional spiritual directors thus become the trainers of the large cadre of "local spiritual directors" who must be developed in our faith communities if spiritual direction is to become available to all who desire it. They coach these people to expand their insights into the dynamics of prayer and discernment.

Professional directors also act as the resource people who handle religious situations which are beyond the capabilities of local people.

**SUMMARY:** Spiritual sharing is a great blessing for noisy contemplation. It can be done with a diary or journal, but it is most effective when at least two or more people regularly share their journeys and celebrate the action of God's spirit in their lives.

All the praying people in a community can then gather periodically to share their faith.

Professionally trained spiritual directors become rich resources, both to train a cadre of local spiritual directors for the community and to handle problems beyond the reach of local resources.

# STUDY QUESTIONS FOR CHAPTER 16

Does keeping a journal help you?

Is there someone around you who might be willing to try noisy contemplation with you? You could become "companions for the journey." Perhaps you could agree to talk once a week for five or six weeks and then decide whether or not to continue.

Is there a trained spiritual director nearby with whom you and your friend(s) can share what is happening as you pray?

# *Merry Prayer*   17

T HE CHAPTER WHICH DWELT upon conflict might seem to deny joy in our lives. It is true that recent centuries of interreligious struggle and the battles with injustice are more marked with angry Christians than with joyful balladeers of the Resurrection. Faith has been a grim business.

Protestants and Roman Catholics squared off. Muslims and Christians sought to send each other to heaven. Christians defended western capitalism from the onslaught of the "godless" communists, and the communists did their best to return the favor.

Laughter and merriment were almost outlawed attitudes distracting from the serious business of worshipping God and protecting the true faith from heretics and unbelievers – sort of like whistling in church.

Our prayer has reflected this seriousness of religious purpose. We sought to close our senses and our hearts to the world in which we live, especially to the struggles. Conflict disturbs our serenity and distracts our focus from the arduous effort to be attentive to God and to the laws and authorities by which God wants us to live.

Like earnest religious adolescents, we've acted as though we had to achieve the work of salvation all by ourselves, with God an over-anxious parent second-guessing every effort.

We have been guilty of the "Atlas Syndrome," where we must hold up our religious world all by ourselves, without relief or even the chance to go to the bathroom. It is no wonder we've often had a pinched look to our religious practice.

Noisy contemplation might moderate that anxiety a bit. It is often marked with a special sign of joy and merriment.

It is the merriment of Pope John XXIII. When asked by a reporter, "How many people work at the Vatican?" he replied: "About half."

It is the merriment of a Cardinal Cushing of Boston. Beginning a Confirmation instruction before nervous children and parents, he would pull out his rosary beads, swing them in a circle and tell about the little girl who did the same while laughing, "Hang on, Jesus. You're going for a ride."

It is the merry perspective of Dorothy Day, the founder of the Catholic Worker movement. For years she was reviled as a suspected communist and a threat to young Catholic people who helped in the soup kitchens.

As she grew old, she became revered as a saintly woman. A reporter asked her how it felt to be respected after the years of suspicion. Dorothy replied, "Everybody loves an old pet."

The joy of noisy contemplation flows from the dawning discovery that signs of God's love lie all around us, even in the midst of our struggles with death and evil.

The merriment bubbles up from the contemplative awareness that we are not alone on our journey of faith.

We travel upon an earth created by a loving God. Our own self is a mirror of this loving Creator. Countless generations have prepared our way. Jesus walked ahead, tested the path and visited our destination – heaven. He told us how our story would turn out – Resurrection.

We travel with numerous sisters and brothers, living and dead, in whose company we are strengthened and can find support when we grow weary or weak (or even angry, as with St. Anthony when he won't find something you have lost and you have to turn his statue to the wall or stick him out in the cold).

In noisy contemplation, we grow in solidarity of hearts with distant sisters and brothers with whom we share efforts to express societal love through structures which are just.

We are not alone, nor do we have to control everything ourselves. We are stronger, more durable and able to live more passionately than we once conceived – tough old crabgrass Christians. Thus we can relax and make merry along the way.

We might recover the wonderful faith of David, whose joy could encourage him to dance before God, even in the face of people who thought such frivolous behavior degrading for a king.

Through the eyes of our prayer we can enter into the paradox of the poor, for whom hope overcomes suffering.

As Gustavo Gutierrez, the liberation theologian, replied to a hostile critic who challenged him for sounding joyful and hopeful when speaking of the suffering endured by the people of Latin America, "The poor of Latin America, like the poor of the earth everywhere, have always suffered and been oppressed. The difference now is that there is hope that this might change. And so, in the midst of suffering their hope is bringing joy."

## STUDY QUESTIONS FOR CHAPTER 17

What do you think of the place of merriment in matters
of prayer and worship?

When does it help or distract?

## LIGHT THE WICK

They said we are to love God
And love our neighbors,
A two-fold command to a lot of lovin'.

But Jesus asks more,
A call to Action
To love our neighbors, near and distant
As ourselves, the oft-forgotten,
A bigger heap of heart-work.

Spiritual people warned us of the road,
'You'll lose the silence,
Swamp the prayer time,
Noisy activists,
Clanging liberation gongs.'

But the Good News is insistent,
'Hear the cry of the poor,
I will be with you all days,'
Crabgrass Christians,
Noisy contemplatives,
Filled with the beatitudes' biases of Jesus.

Who behold creation with the eyes of their hearts
'Til wax and wick are used up.
Whose life cries out,

'PEGA LA MECHA' *

— WRC 2008

* *colloquial Nicaraguan expression meaning 'light the wick'*

# Conclusion

THE GOAL OF NOISY CONTEMPLATION is to encourage us to trust and "own" our experience of God's Spirit at work in our daily living, to celebrate the gifts God has placed in us and to develop habits of contemplation that nourish our hearts with a love drawn from every dimension of our lives.

Noisy contemplation stretches prayer to include, not only our quest for direct encounter with God, but each dimension of the great commandment.

We can use noisy contemplation to bond with God directly, with Jesus in the Scriptures and in the Eucharist and with the Spirit of God working in our hearts.

We can use noisy contemplation to see ourselves with a prayerful gaze somewhat like that with which God beholds us.

We can bond with neighbors who are near and dear to us and we can use contemplation to build bridges of reconciliation when love faces conflict or is broken.

This prayer adds contemplative wings to our hearts so that we experience and bond with sisters and brothers who are distant, but whose story, whether told by TV, radio, the morning paper or some other channel to our imagination, can touch us. Social love can nurture us in Dorothy Solle's "revolutionary patience," the persevering love needed to nurture justice upon the earth.

*Signs & Songs of Prayer*

As noisy contemplation grows, what will you find?

You will discover new beauty in the world around you. Your habit of contemplating the earth will serve up daily moments of wonder and discovery, even for city dwellers who can rejoice in the crabgrass through the cracks in the pavement.

You will discover people throughout your daily lives and share some of Jesus' joy in beholding God's people and finding them deeply lovable. You will enter more deeply into the Scriptures, not just to know them, but to savor the experiences described and be more able to bring the spirit of Jesus alive into your daily living.

From contemplating yourself, you will become more honest and truthful about who you are and who you are called to become. You will grow encouraged to leave behind the baggage of self-rejection and to walk lightly in the adult confidence that the person whom God created and loves is worthy of your love as well.

From contemplating distant neighbors your arms will grow long and strong enough to embrace them. Social justice will no longer be the special work of a few Christians but the societal love of all believers, a sign that our faith is growing mature.

And, in the midst of it all, you who become noisy contemplatives will be marked by a growing merriment in love that puts your struggles against the perspective of Jesus, whose Spirit of love walks with us and shares the burdens.

We travel with a God who loves us. We travel with a community of faith. We'll often remember that we're crabgrass Christians, whose love can survive in the cracks of life's sidewalks. Our love reminds us that God's Spirit is with us all days. We are blessed with a merry God – indeed, we are the entertainment.

## STUDY QUESTIONS FOR CONCLUSION

What has happened to your ideas on prayer from reading about and experimenting with noisy contemplation?

What did you like least?

What did you like most?

Have you grown more hopeful that, with the help of God's Spirit, you can pray more deeply?

# About the Author

WILLIAM R. CALLAHAN is a codirector of the Quixote Center in Brentwood, Maryland. Formerly a physicist who did his doctoral work at Johns Hopkins University, he was ordained as a Jesuit priest in 1965. In 1971, he was part of the founding team of the Center of Concern in Washington, DC. In 1975 he began Priests for Equality, and with Dolores C. Pomerleau he cofounded the Quixote Center.

In recent years, Bill has coordinated the Quest for Peace campaign which sends development and humanitarian aid to Nicaragua. In 1991, he was dismissed from the Jesuit order, apparently for his advocacy on sensitive issues of justice within the church such as gender equality, gospel treatment of gay and lesbian people and for his work to end the repression of the people of Central America.

Bill links his spirituality and social consciousness, nurtures equality in civil society and the Roman Catholic church. He works, speaks and writes on Central America and Haiti and encourages Catholics to share responsibility for the life of the Church. Bill, a lover of the earth and its people, is a longtime farmer and beekeeper.

Bill welcomes your thoughts via e-mail to noco@quixote.org.

# About the Quixote Center

A gathering of people
who work and pray
with laughter,
to reach for stars
that seem too distant to be touched,
or too dim to be worth the effort.

We try to be friends
with people in need,
and to celebrate life
with people who believe
that the struggle to be like Jesus
in building a world more justly loving
is worth the gift of our lives.

*Learn more about the Quixote Center
and its programs at quixote.org*

## THE INCLUSIVE BIBLE – THE FIRST EGALITARIAN TRANSLATION

After an 18-year effort, the Quixote Center's inclusive-language translation of the Bible has been published by Sheed & Ward in a single, beautiful volume. *The Inclusive Bible* is a fresh, dynamic translation of the Bible into modern English, carefully crafted to let the power and poetry of the language shine forth. Many long-term supporters have expressed their joy for this Bible that finds new and nonsexist ways to express the same ancient truths*. Readers are finding in *The Inclusive Bible* a re-imagining of the Scriptures and our relationship to them.

## INCLUSIVE SUNDAY LECTIONARIES

Our popular *Inclusive Sunday Lectionaries and Responsorial Psalms* in Cycles A, B and C are completely redesigned for easier oral reading, along with updated inclusive language texts. Many universities, seminaries, intentional communities and mainline denominations have been using them for the last ten years.

## NOISY CONTEMPLATION:
## DEEP PRAYER FOR BUSY PEOPLE

This classic of contemporary spirituality – which has sold over 100,000 copies – is newly revised for the 21st century. You'll find chapters on how Jesus practiced Noisy Contemplation, marks of healthy prayer, contemplation amid conflict, the spirituality of social justice, the joys of "merry prayer" and more.

*Noisy Contemplation* will help busy people everywhere cultivate a more contemplative life.

## RIVERS OF HOPE

In 2007, the Quest for Peace published *Rivers of Hope*, an account from our Nicaraguan partners of the 20+ years of South-North partnership with the Institute of John XXIII. We've added our own tales and published the book as a tabloid newspaper to make it available to everyone who has who has shared the Quest.

A Quest friend wrote: "*Rivers of Hope* just amazed me — the long-term, deep work you and your partners in Nicaragua have been committed to. Wow! I just had no idea. It's a terrific story of hope."

*More information on the Web at quixote.org*

# ORDER FORM

*order online at quixote.org*

| ITEM | | QTY | PRICE | SHIPPING | ITEM TOTAL |
|---|---|---|---|---|---|
| *The Inclusive Bible – The First Egalitarian Translation* hardcover, 808 pages | | | $ 33 <br> *17% off cover* | $4 ea. | |
| *Sunday Inclusive Language Lectionaries with Responsorial Psalms* 8½ × 11, spiral bound | CYCLE A <br> CYCLE B <br> CYCLE C | | 1 book – $ 45 <br> 2 books – $ 80 <br> 3 books – $ 115 | $4 ea. | |
| *Noisy Contemplation: Deep Prayer for Busy People* by William Callahan softcover, 192 pages | | | 1 copy   $ 15 <br> 2–5 copies   $13 <br> 6–10 copies   $11 <br> 11–25 copies   $9 | $3 <br> $2 ea. <br> $1 ea. <br> $1 ea. | |
| *Rivers of Hope: Two Decades of Solidarity Between the Quixote Center and the Institute of John XXIII* tabloid newspaper format | | | $ 5 <br> *bulk discounts available – please call* | *free* | |
| | | | | SUBTOTAL | |
| | | | | TAX-DEDUCTIBLE DONATION *thank you!* | |
| | | | | TOTAL | |

## SHIPPING ADDRESS

Name

Address

City      State      Zip

## METHOD OF PAYMENT

☐ Check enclosed    ☐ Mastercard    ☐ VISA    ☐ AMEX

## CREDIT CARD INFORMATION
*please print legibly!*

Name on card

Card no.      Exp

Signature

Phone

Credit card billing address

City      State      Zip

Detach and mail to:

Quixote Center Publications
PO BOX 5206
Hyattsville, MD 20782

*For assistance call 800 746 1160*